AWESOME ADVENTURES AT THE SMITHSONIAN

The Official Kids Guide to the Smithsonian Institution

EMILY B. KORRELL

Smithsonian Books
Washington, DC

This 1909 Wright Military Flyer is the world's first military airplane.

TABLE OF CONTENTS

The Star-Spangled Banner is America's flag, national anthem, and a legendary story all rolled into one.

Phoenix, a North Atlantic right whale, is one of the largest mammals on Earth.

WELCOME!

Congratulations! You've made it to Washington, DC, the home of the world famous Smithsonian Institution. Are you ready for a great adventure? Prepare to be amazed at all there is to see and do in the museums of the Smithsonian!

How to use this guide

The museums are **BIG PLACES**, full of fascinating treasures. You could spend an entire year exploring the **SMITHSONIAN MUSEUMS** and still not see all there is to see. Of course, you probably don't have a year to explore the museums, so you need to make sure you don't miss the Smithsonian's **MOST AMAZING TREASURES** on your visit. *Awesome Adventures at the Smithsonian: The Official Kids Guide to the Smithsonian Institution* will point you in the right direction and help you figure out what you really want to see.

Awesome Adventures at the Smithsonian is packed full of fun information and activities created just for you! It features three of the Smithsonian Institution's museums: the **NATIONAL AIR AND SPACE MUSEUM**, the **NATIONAL MUSEUM OF NATURAL HISTORY**, and the **NATIONAL MUSEUM OF AMERICAN HISTORY**. These are three of the most visited museums in the world!

Each museum has a section, and each section has interesting information about the main exhibits in each museum. There are also **ACTIVITIES** for you to do either while visiting these exhibits or at home. Even if you don't make it to an exhibit, this guide will help you find **ONLINE RESOURCES** and activities so you can still experience the treasures after you've left the museums!

ACTIVITIES TO DO

This guide is your ticket to fun and adventure in the museums. It's YOUR book, so go ahead and:

- Write in it using pencil!
- Draw in it using pencil!
- Read about the things that make you curious.
- Try the activities. Some you can do right in the museums; some you can do at home.
- Use the museum maps and the pictures to figure out your own "Must-See" list.
- Explore the website for even more fun activities, stories, and information about your favorite Smithsonian discoveries.

MUSEUM DOs & DON'Ts

Museum DOs

- Plan your visit—use *The Official Kids Guide* to help you.
- Dress comfortably and travel light—this will help you enjoy your visit.
- Take breaks—give your brain a chance to think about all you are seeing.
- Ask questions—docents, who are museum educators, are there to help answer your questions.
- Share the space with other visitors—mind your manners and use your indoor voice.
- Take photos—photography is allowed in the Smithsonian museums.

Museum DON'Ts

- Don't touch, climb, or ride on a museum exhibit, unless it's a "hands-on" exhibit.
- Don't write with pens.
- No food in the museums please. Eat outside or in the cafeterias only.
- No horsing around in the museums!
- Don't bring your toys, games, or pets.
- Don't try to see everything in one day. Take your time in a few exhibits rather than rushing through them all.

CHECK IT OUT!

DO YOU WANT TO FIND OUT MORE ABOUT YOUR FAVORITE SMITHSONIAN FINDS? ARE YOU LOOKING FOR MORE FUN ACTIVITIES LIKE THE ONES IN THIS GUIDE? CHECK OUT *AWESOME ADVENTURES AT THE SMITHSONIAN: THE OFFICIAL KIDS GUIDE TO THE SMITHSONIAN INSTITUTION* WEBSITE. THERE YOU WILL FIND FUN FACTS, STORIES, GAMES, ACTIVITIES, AND LINKS TO SMITHSONIAN TREASURES ONLINE.

WHAT IS THAT?

THIS STRANGE LOOKING SQUARE IS CALLED A QR CODE. IF YOU SCAN IT WITH A SMART PHONE YOU WILL BE TAKEN DIRECTLY TO THE RELATED WEB SITE. PRETTY COOL, HUH? WHAT IF YOU DON'T HAVE A SMART PHONE? NO PROBLEM! ALL OF THE WEB SITES ARE LISTED IN ADDITIONAL RESOURCES ON P.126.

THINGS TO SEE AND DO AT THE NATIONAL AIR AND SPACE MUSEUM:

☐ See the Apollo 11 command module, *Columbia*, which took the first astronauts to the moon and brought them home, in *Milestones of Flight* (Gallery 100).

☐ Touch a real moon rock brought back by Apollo astronauts in *Milestones of Flight* (Gallery 100).

☐ See what it was like to fly in the 1950s by boarding a Douglas DC-7, an early passenger airplane in *America by Air* (Gallery 102).

☐ Try out dozens of hands-on activities and climb aboard a Cessna 150 airplane in *How Things Fly* (Gallery 109).

☐ Design your own space station module and be the flight director of a space mission in *Moving Beyond Earth* (Gallery 113).

☐ See the original Wright Flyer—the world's first airplane—in *The Wright Brothers & the Invention of the Aerial Age* (Gallery 209).

☐ Walk through the Skylab orbital workshop and get a feel for what it's like to live and work in space (Gallery 114).

☐ Visit the museum's observatory, which has telescopes where you can observe the sun during the day (four days a week) and at special times in the evenings to see the planets and stars (East Terrace, weather permitting).

☐ Take an unforgettable journey into the night sky and the cosmos beyond in the Albert Einstein Planetarium (entrance fee).

☐ Experience a larger-than-life movie about flight in the Lockheed Martin IMAX® Theater (entrance fee).

The P-51 Mustang was one of the best fighter planes of World War II.

WELCOME TO THE NATIONAL AIR AND SPACE MUSEUM

You have arrived at one of the most popular museums on Earth, the Smithsonian **NATIONAL AIR AND SPACE MUSEUM**. Here you will be surrounded by the world's largest collection of airplanes and spacecraft. You will also discover all kinds of objects—large and small—related to the science and technology of flight, the study of space, and the exploration of the universe. Here you will spend a lot of time looking up at the planes and spacecraft that seem to be flying throughout this huge museum.

Have you ever flown on a plane? **WOULD YOU LIKE TO VISIT OUTER SPACE SOMEDAY?** It may be hard to believe, but human flight is a relatively new development. In the past 100 years or so, people have figured out how to get off the ground into the air and stay in the air. And it's only been about 60 years since people figured out how to travel to space.

Your grandparents probably watched the first humans walk on the moon on television. Ask them to tell you about it!

YOU ARE LUCKY TO LIVE IN THE AGE OF FLIGHT! Our big world seems smaller today since we can fly almost anywhere on Earth within a day. Where would you like to fly? How about space? Maybe in your lifetime, spaceflight will become common for many people, not just astronauts. Would you like to take a space vacation?

So, get started with your exploration of flight and space travel. At the National Air and Space Museum you will find out how it all began, what important steps were taken along the way, and **WHAT LIES AHEAD FOR EXPLORERS LIKE YOU!**

JOURNAL

It's a bird! It's a plane!

What are you most excited to see at the National Air and Space Museum?

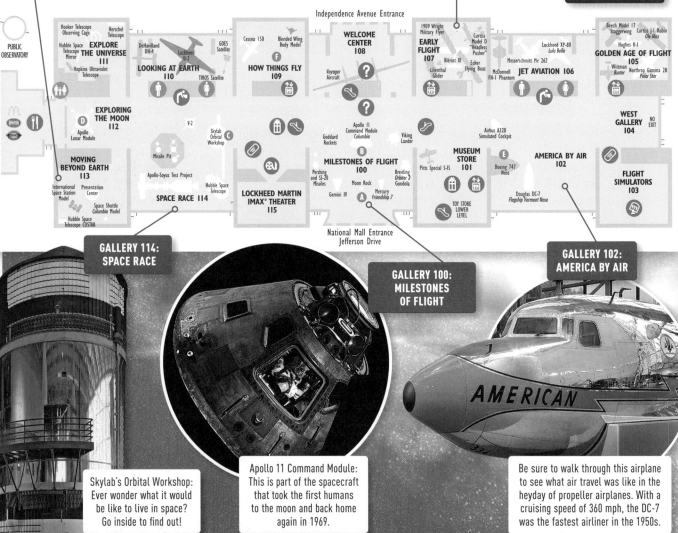

PUBLIC OBSERVATORY

Hooker Telescope Observing Cage
Herschel Telescope
Hubble Space Telescope Mirror
EXPLORE THE UNIVERSE 111
Hopkins Ultraviolet Telescope

DeHavilland DH-4
Lockheed U-2
LOOKING AT EARTH 110
GOES Satellite
TIROS Satellite

Cessna 150
Blended Wing Body Model
HOW THINGS FLY 109
Voyager Aircraft

Independence Avenue Entrance

WELCOME CENTER 108

1909 Wright Military Flyer
EARLY FLIGHT 107
Curtiss Model D "Headless Pusher"
Blériot XI
Lilienthal Glider
Ecker Flying Boat

Curtiss J-1 Robin *Ole Miss*
Beech Model 17 Staggerwing
Hughes H-1
GOLDEN AGE OF FLIGHT 105
Lockheed XP-80 *Lulu Belle*
Messerschmitt Me 262
McDonnell FH-1 Phantom
JET AVIATION 106
Wittman Buster
Northrop Gamma 2B *Polar Star*

EXPLORING THE MOON 112
Apollo Lunar Module

V-2

Skylab Orbital Workshop

Goddard Rockets
Apollo 11 Command Module *Columbia*
Viking Lander

Airbus A320 Simulated Cockpit

WEST GALLERY 104
NO EXIT

AMERICA BY AIR 102

MOVING BEYOND EARTH 113
International Space Station Model
Presentation Center

Missile Pit

Apollo-Soyuz Test Project

Hubble Space Telescope

Space Shuttle *Columbia* Model
Hubble Space Telescope COSTAR

SPACE RACE 114

Pershing and SS-20 Missiles
Gemini IV
MILESTONES OF FLIGHT 100
Moon Rock
Mercury *Friendship 7*
Breitling *Orbiter 3* Gondola

Pitts Special S-1S
MUSEUM STORE 101
Boeing 747 Nose
Douglas DC-7 *Flagship Vermont* Nose

AMERICA BY AIR 102

FLIGHT SIMULATORS 103

LOCKHEED MARTIN IMAX® THEATER 115

TOY STORE LOWER LEVEL

National Mall Entrance
Jefferson Drive

GALLERY 114: SPACE RACE

GALLERY 100: MILESTONES OF FLIGHT

GALLERY 102: AMERICA BY AIR

Skylab's Orbital Workshop: Ever wonder what it would be like to live in space? Go inside to find out!

Apollo 11 Command Module: This is part of the spacecraft that took the first humans to the moon and back home again in 1969.

Be sure to walk through this airplane to see what air travel was like in the heyday of propeller airplanes. With a cruising speed of 360 mph, the DC-7 was the fastest airliner in the 1950s.

AIR AND SPACE MUSEUM

Lockheed 5B Vega: Amelia Earhart piloted this streamlined, red airplane when she flew alone across the Atlantic Ocean in 1932.

Mitsubishi A6M5 Zero: Go nose-to-nose with fighter planes from World War II.

GALLERY 208: PIONEERS OF FLIGHT

GALLERY 205: WORLD WAR II AVIATION

SECOND FLOOR

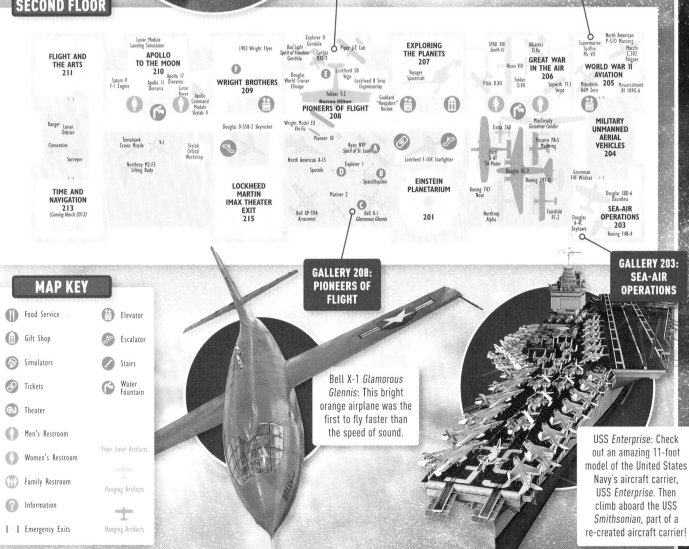

FLIGHT AND THE ARTS
211

APOLLO TO THE MOON
210

Lunar Module Landing Simulation

Saturn V F-1 Engine

Apollo 11 Diorama

Apollo 17 Diorama

Lunar Rover

Apollo Command Module Skylab 4

Ranger

Lunar Orbiter

Clementine

Surveyor

Tomahawk Cruise Missile

V-1

Northrop M2-F3 Lifting Body

Skylab Orbital Workshop

TIME AND NAVIGATION
213
(Coming March 2013)

1903 Wright Flyer

WRIGHT BROTHERS
209

Douglas World Cruiser Chicago

Bud Light Spirit of Freedom Gondola

Explorer II Gondola

Curtiss R3C-2

Piper J-2 Cub

Lockheed 5B Vega

Lockheed 8 Sirus Tingmissartoq

Fokker T-2

Barron Hilton
PIONEERS OF FLIGHT
208

Wright Model EX Vin Fiz

Douglas D-55B-2 Skyrocket

Goddard "Hoopskirt" Rocket

Pioneer 10

Ryan NYP Spirit of St. Louis

North American X-15

Explorer 1

Sputnik

SpaceShipOne

Mariner 2

LOCKHEED MARTIN IMAX THEATER
EXIT
215

Bell XP-59A Airacomet

Bell X-1 Glamorous Glennis

EXPLORING THE PLANETS
207

Voyager Spacecraft

Lockheed F-104 Starfighter

EINSTEIN PLANETARIUM
201

SPAD XIII Smith IV

Albatros D.Va

Voisin VIII

Pfalz D.XII

Fokker D.VII

GREAT WAR IN THE AIR
206

Sopwith 7F.1 Snipe

North American P-51D Mustang

Supermarine Spitfire Mk. VII

Macchi C.202 Folgore

WORLD WAR II AVIATION
205

Mitsubishi A6M Zero

Messerschmitt Bf 109G-6

MacCready Gossamer Condor

Extra 260

Ford 5-AT Tri-Motor

Pitcairn PA-5 Mailwing

Douglas DC-3

Boeing 247-D

Boeing 747 Nose

Northrop Alpha

Fairchild FC-2

MILITARY UNMANNED AERIAL VEHICLES
204

Grumman F4F Wildcat

Douglas SBD-6 Dauntless

SEA-AIR OPERATIONS
203

Douglas A-4C Skyhawk

Boeing F4B-4

GALLERY 208: PIONEERS OF FLIGHT

GALLERY 203: SEA-AIR OPERATIONS

MAP KEY

- 🍴 Food Service
- 🎁 Gift Shop
- 🎮 Simulators
- 🎟 Tickets
- 🎭 Theater
- 🚹 Men's Restroom
- 🚺 Women's Restroom
- 👪 Family Restroom
- ❓ Information
- |↔| Emergency Exits

- 🛗 Elevator
- Escalator
- Stairs
- 🚰 Water Fountain

Floor Level Artifacts

Hanging Artifacts

Hanging Artifacts

Bell X-1 Glamorous Glennis: This bright orange airplane was the first to fly faster than the speed of sound.

USS Enterprise: Check out an amazing 11-foot model of the United States Navy's aircraft carrier, USS Enterprise. Then climb aboard the USS Smithsonian, part of a re-created aircraft carrier!

VISIT THE
HOW THINGS FLY
GALLERY ONLINE.

This is an image of an airfoil, which is a cross section, or side view, of an airplane wing.

TRY THIS IN THE MUSEUM!

Now that you know more about how airplanes actually fly, take a closer look at the planes "FLYING AROUND" in the National Air and Space Museum. See if you can answer the questions on the right.

- Check out the wing shape on different airplanes. Do you notice the curved tops?
- What materials make up each plane? Are they heavy or lightweight?
- Look at the shape of the airplanes. Which planes do you think have less drag?
- Figure out what gives each plane its thrust—propellers, jet engines, or rocket engines?

Think of releasing an inflated balloon and watching it zoom through the air—that's a good example of thrust!

The DC-3's streamlined, versatile design and strong wing construction made it an exceptional aircraft.

Jet engine

THRUST

Thrust is the force that **PUSHES** a plane forward. Airplanes use engines to produce thrust. Three kinds of engines power most planes: piston, jet, and rocket.

Piston engines cannot produce thrust on their own, so they provide power to a propeller. The spinning propeller creates higher pressure behind the propeller and lower pressure in front. This pressure difference pushes the plane forward. Jet engines and rocket engines produce thrust by increasing the pressure inside the engine. The increased pressure in the engine exerts more pressure forward than it does backward. This pressure difference also pushes the plane forward.

You can see the effect of thrust when you blow up a balloon and release it without tying the end. The balloon flies forward while the air inside escapes in the opposite direction, just like the exhaust of a jet or rocket engine.

WEIGHT

Thanks to gravity, weight is the force that **PULLS** a plane down. The lighter a plane is, the less lift it needs to get off the ground. That's why airplane designers use lightweight, but strong materials and structures to keep planes as light as possible.

The plane below looks like it's made completely out of metal, right? But it isn't. The body of the plane is actually made out of hollow steel tubing – strong, but lightweight – and the wing is made out of spruce – a strong type of wood – covered in cotton fabric and painted silver!

The *Spirit of St. Louis*

DRAG

Drag is the force that **PUSHES** back against a plane. Drag is caused by friction and air pressure differences.

You can feel this force when you move your hand through water. Try this in a pool or the tub. Put your hand into the water with your fingers pointed straight down. Move your hand through the water really fast, with your palm facing forward. Do you feel the pressure of the water pushing against your palm? That's drag. Now, put your hand out flat, palm down, so it is parallel to the bottom. Move your hand back and forth really fast. Do you notice how there is **LESS DRAG** this way? That's because when your hand is parallel to the bottom it is a more streamlined, or smoother, shape, which allows it to move more easily through the water.

Propeller

CREATE YOUR OWN

TRY THIS AT HOME!

Create your own flight lab to see **WHICH PAPER AIRPLANE DESIGNS WILL FLY THE FARTHEST.**

Gliders fly without engines, just like paper airplanes!

What would happen if you altered a plane's lift, weight, drag or thrust? Could it fly faster or further, or do stunts? Try experimenting with the forces of flight at home.

Here's what you will need:

REGULAR PRINTER PAPER (8½ X 11 INCHES)

COMPUTER WITH INTERNET ACCESS AND A PRINTER

PAPER CLIPS

TIP!
FOR AN EARTH FRIENDLY PROJECT REUSE PAPER THAT HAS ALREADY BEEN PRINTED ON.

CHOOSE YOUR AIRPLANE DESIGN HERE!
SOME ARE EASY TO MAKE; OTHERS ARE MORE DIFFICULT. TAKE YOUR PICK! YOU CAN EVEN CHOOSE COLORFUL DESIGNS TO ADD TO YOUR PLANE. PRINT OUT YOUR CHOICE AND FOLD YOUR AIRPLANE ACCORDING TO THE INSTRUCTIONS. MAKE ONE, TWO, OR ALL THREE!

STOPWATCH AND A FRIEND TO TIME YOUR TEST FLIGHTS

NOTEBOOK AND PENCIL TO RECORD YOUR FLIGHT DATA

The Dart
(EASY)

DESCRIPTION: The Dart is very streamlined, with a long fuselage (body) and delta wing (a wing shape like a triangle).

CHARACTERISTICS: The Dart is excellent for long-distance flights and flights requiring accuracy but it's not very good for stunts. The Dart is an extremely fast and stable paper airplane.

FLIGHT LAB

Does this stealth bomber look like any of the paper airplanes below?

The Canard
(MEDIUM)

DESCRIPTION: The Canard has a long fuselage, delta wing, and canard. A canard is a small wing that is in front of an airplane's main wing.

CHARACTERISTICS: The Canard is excellent for long-distance flights and flights requiring accuracy. Its forward wings give extra control over how it flies. The Canard is not nearly as fast as the Dart, but it is fairly stable.

The Delta
(HARD)

DESCRIPTION: The Delta has a wide delta wing, winglets (turned-up wings), and a blunt nose.

CHARACTERISTICS: The Delta is a slow-moving glider. Its forward weight design and large tapered winglets make it a stable flier. If built right and launched from a high place, it can make long, sweeping turns.

Once you have your paper airplane ready, **SET UP A TEST AREA**. It's best if you can test your airplane outside, on a non-windy day. Mark your starting point. Always throw your plane from the same point. Be sure to do the same test many times. Scientists always write down their test results, so have your pencil and notebook handy!

You can test different things in your flight lab:

- See how long your plane stays in the air. Test it at least three times. Use a stopwatch and write down your results.
- See how far your plane flies. Use a tape measure or yard stick to measure each flight.
- You can also make slight changes to your plane's design to see what happens.

Here are some suggestions for ways to change your design:

- Angle the rear wings up, just a little bit, with small folds. What happens? Why do you think so?
- Angle the rear wings down, just a little bit, with small folds. What happens? Why do you think so?
- Add a paper clip to the underside of the plane. Place it near the front of the plane. What happens? Try it again, moving it back a bit. Continue to test it out, placing the paper clip in different spots. Think about how it changes the flight of the plane each time.
- Make up your own experiments. Try folding a different kind of paper airplane. Once you come up with a design, make one small change for each flight and watch what happens.

JOURNAL

What did you figure out about flight in your flight lab?

How do these different adjustments affect the way lift, weight, drag, and thrust act on your paper airplane?

WHO'S WHO IN EARLY FLIGHT

When the Age of Flight began, there were many "firsts" waiting to be accomplished.

Feats like being the first person to fly across the country, or across an ocean, called out to early pilots. With a lot of practice and courage, some pilots became famous heroes for their firsts. **HERE ARE A FEW FAMOUS EARLY FLIERS.**

1903

Wright Brothers' Flying Machine a Success!

After years of research and experimentation, two brothers from Dayton, Ohio, Wilbur and Orville Wright, have achieved human flight! The brothers' flying machine, the Wright Flyer, took off at Kitty Hawk, North Carolina, on the morning of December 17, 1903. Powered by a small engine and piloted by younger brother, Orville, the flyer flew a mere 12 seconds and covered a distance of 120 feet. It was a short journey, indeed; but it was the first sustained, powered, contolled flight of an object heavier-than-air. Thanks to the teamwork of these remarkable brothers, we may now be entering a brave new age of flight!

Orville and Wilbur Wright—what a team!

1911

It's Official! Cal Rodgers First Person to Fly across the United States

After 49 days of flying and only 16 crashes along the way, Cal Rodgers landed his single-seat airplane in Pasadena, California. His airplane, manufactured by the Wright Company, was named for a new brand of grape soda, the *Vin Fiz*. Despite needing to be repaired and rebuilt many times during the trip, the *Vin Fiz* made it from Sheepshead Bay, New York, all the way to the Pacific Ocean. Rodgers set off on his exciting journey in hopes of winning a prize offered by publisher William Randolph Hearst. The prize would go to the first person to fly across the country in 30 days. Though Rodgers was not fast enough to win the prize, he still made history by becoming the first person to fly across the United States!

Nothing could stop daredevil Cal Rodgers!

1921

Queen Bess Thrills Crowds

Flying in her Curtiss Jenny, aviatrix Bessie Coleman continues to thrill crowds with her daring stunt flying. Coleman dreamed of flying from the time she was a little girl in Texas. Unfortunately, because she is African American, no one in the United States would train her, so she headed to flight school in France. She is the first licensed African American pilot and is amazing audiences far and wide. She is so popular that her adoring fans call her "Queen Bess."

Barnstorming Bessie Coleman—one fearless aviatrix!

TRY THIS IN THE MUSEUM!

Find out about the famous firsts of flight, and see if you can match them with their aircraft. Check off each plane that you can find in the *PIONEERS OF FLIGHT GALLERY*.

N-X-211 RYAN

Spirit of St.Louis

1927
Charles Lindbergh First to Cross Atlantic Solo

"Lucky Lindy" has landed in Paris, France, becoming the first person to fly solo across the Atlantic Ocean. On May 20, 1927, he departed New York and flew his airplane, the *Spirit of St. Louis*, all the way to Paris, France. After a 33½-hour flight, Lindbergh and his silver aircraft were greeted by over 100,000 people. He became an overnight sensation and set off an aviation craze—suddenly everyone wants to fly!

1933
Anne and Charles Lindbergh Conquer the World

The Lindberghs have returned from their second global expedition. The husband-and-wife team has flown all over the world looking for good airline routes. Anne served as Charles' copilot and radio operator in their aircraft *Tingmissartoq*. The airplane received its fancy name from an Inuit boy in Greenland. The name makes sense. It means: "one who flies like a big bird."

CHECK IT OUT!
PACK FOR A LONG, ADVENTUROUS FLIGHT, DESIGN AN AIR RACER, FLY AROUND THE WORLD, AND MEET MORE TRAILBLAZING PILOTS AT *THE PIONEERS OF FLIGHT* ONLINE GALLERY.

1937
Aviatrix, Amelia Earhart, Missing

Amelia Earhart's plane disappeared over the Pacific Ocean during the last leg of her round-the-world journey. Earhart was attempting to become the first person to fly around the world. She had already set a number of flying records, including being the first woman to fly alone across the Atlantic Ocean in 1932. She was also the first woman to fly by herself non-stop across the United States. Now, the question is this: What has happened to the fearless aviatrix, Amelia Earhart? We may never know.

That was one long flight for Charles Lindbergh.

Anne Lindbergh—always up for an adventure.

Amelia Earhart nearly completed her round-the-world flight.

15

William "Wild Bill" Hopson was an air mail pilot in the 1920s. He earned the nickname "Wild Bill" for his fast and fearless flying.

it could take many days, or weeks, for a letter to travel by train or truck to its destination across the country. In 1918, the US government decided to get the mail flying. By doing this, they set up air routes not only for mail, but also for paying passengers someday in the future.

YOU BE THE PILOT!
SEE WHAT IT WAS LIKE TO FLY THE MAIL IN 1920 IN A CURTISS JENNY.

Flying the mail was a dangerous job! What do you think went wrong here?

1927–1941

By the late 1920s, privately owned airlines began flying passengers around the country. They used the same safe flying routes that were mapped out for the airmail program. Not just anybody could fly, though. Air travel was really expensive! A one-way, cross-country airline ticket could cost about as much as a new car at the time! Also, air travel was often uncomfortable. In bad weather it was an extremely loud and very bumpy ride.

By the late 1930s, planes that carried passengers—called airliners—started to improve. The newer aircraft were larger, faster, safer, and more comfortable. Gradually, more passengers started flying, but it was still very expensive to fly. Female flight attendants began serving passengers on many airlines. Although airline travel was becoming more popular and was considered adventurous, it was still far from comfortable. Flying in low altitudes, bouncing through wind and weather, often made passengers sick.

"The airplanes smell of hot oil and simmering aluminum, disinfectant, feces, leather, and puke...the stewardesses, short-tempered and reeking of vomit..."

Ernest K. Gann, *an early commercial pilot*

THE BUSINESS OF AIR TRAVEL

SEE WHAT IT WAS LIKE TO TRAVEL IN THE 1950S! CLIMB ABOARD A DC-7 IN *AMERICA BY AIR* (GALLERY 102), OR EXPLORE A MODEL ONLINE.

1941–1958

After World War II, new and improved airliners made their appearance in the skies. These new airplanes were much larger, faster, and more comfortable than earlier airplanes. The cost of plane tickets started dropping, making air travel affordable for more and more people. In 1955, air travel became more popular than train travel in the United States. Air travel was something many people felt they could not live without.

The Douglas DC-7 was a popular propeller airliner in the 1950s.

The Boeing 247 was the first modern airliner.

1958–TODAY

In the late 1950s, a new kind of aircraft was introduced—the jet. Slow propeller airplanes were replaced by high-speed planes with powerful jet engines. Traveling from one side of the United States to the other took only five hours. Plane travel was comfortable in these large jets, which could carry hundreds of passengers.

The jet engine made air travel faster, cheaper, and more popular than ever.

FLYING FACT! TODAY, PEOPLE ARE FLYING MORE THAN EVER. HAVE YOU TRAVELED ON AN AIRPLANE?

CHECK IT OUT! PLAY THE "BAGGAGE CLAIM GAME" TO SEE WHAT PEOPLE ARE TAKING WITH THEM ON BOARD PLANES.

Flight attendants in the 1960s had some imaginative uniforms. This one included a bubble helmet to protect the flight attendant's hairdo!

IN THE MUSEUM! GALLERIES 104, 107, 203, 205, and 206 to find the planes you see here.

A TIMELINE OF

Lighter-than-air craft (balloons) were used in wars even before the Wright brothers flew their first plane. Every major war has led to the development of faster and more capable aircraft. **FOLLOW THE TIMELINE** below to see how military aviation has developed over the years.

The P-51 Mustang protected large Air Force bombers on long missions.

During the Civil War, balloons were used to gain a view from above.

Thousands of biplane fighters, like this German Albatros, served in WWI. It is one of two that survive today.

1861 | **1909** | **1914–1918** | **1941–1945** | **1946–1989**

The American Civil War

Did you know gas-filled balloons were used during the American Civil War? Both the Union and Confederate armies used balloons for reconnaissance during the Civil War, marking the first time that balloons were used in the United States.

First Military Flyer

The world's first military airplane was bought by the US Army from the Wright brothers on August 2, 1909, at the cost of $30,000. You can see the Wright Military Flyer in the *Early Flight* gallery (Gallery 107).

World War I

At the start of World War I, the use of military airplanes was still new in warfare. When the United States entered the war in 1917, it had only a few dozen outdated planes. By the end of the war in 1918, it had built thousands of new planes.

World War II

The P-51 Mustang was one of the best fighters of World War II. It was fast, agile, and carried great fire power. It was used for reconnaissance, escorting (flying alongside bombers to protect them), as well as attacking ground targets.

Cold War

The SR-71 Blackbird was made to fly on superfast, high-altitude reconnaissance missions. It remains one of the world's fastest airplanes. In 1990, it flew from California to Washington, DC, in just over an hour! This aircraft can be seen at the Steven F. Udvar-Hazy Center.

10 FACTS!
LEARN 10 IMPRESSIVE FACTS ABOUT THE BLACKBIRD.

This 1909 Wright Military Flyer is the world's first military airplane.

This 1964 SR-71 Blackbird is made mostly of the strong, lightweight metal titanium.

AIRCRAFT AT WAR

The F-86 Sabre's angled wings made it easier to control at high speeds.

The US Air Force, Navy, and Marine Corps flew F-4 Phantoms for decades.

The unmanned RQ-7 Shadow can be launched by a catapult and flies missions day or night.

1950-1953	1964-1975	1990-1991	2001–PRESENT (AS OF 2012)	2003-2011

Korean War

The F-86 Sabre was America's first swept-wing fighter jet. Its wings were angled back towards its tail, making it easier to control. It was capable of flying near the speed of sound. You can see it at the Steven F. Udvar-Hazy Center.

Vietnam War (official US involvement)

The record-breaking McDonnell F-4 Phantom flew combat and air patrol missions in Vietnam. For a long time it was the fastest, highest-flying, longest-range jet available. You can see the F-4 Phantom in the Boeing Aviation Hangar at the Steven F. Udvar-Hazy Center.

Operation Desert Storm

The RQ-2 Pioneer carries no pilot—it is a small unmanned aerial vehicle, or UAV, controlled by people on the ground. UAVs, like the Pioneer, are used for reconnaissance (gathering information before battle), watching enemies, and collecting battle damage information. The Pioneer was used during the Gulf War. After flying its mission, it could be recovered by flying into a large net aboard a ship or by catching its tail hook on land.

Operation Enduring Freedom

The MQ-1 Predator, has proven itself to be an important UAV. It flew reconnaissance and attack missions over Afghanistan after the 9/11 terrorist attacks in 2001. It was the first UAV in history to fire missiles against enemy forces.

The MQ-1 Predator is the first unmanned aircraft capable of launching missiles over enemy territory.

Operation Iraqi Freedom

The RQ-7A Shadow is a UAV that flew missions over Iraq. Flown by controllers on the ground, it could fly reconnaissance missions day or night. When you see the RQ-7 Shadow and other UAVs in the *Military Unmanned Vehicles* exhibit (Gallery 104), you may be shocked at the small size of these aircraft.

The unmanned RQ-2 Pioneer was operated from the battleship *Wisconsin* during Operation Desert Storm in 1991.

THE
TUS[
AIR
Read all abou
American pilots
during World Wa
a section in F
(Gall

Col. Benjamin O. Davis Jr. in the cockpit of his P-51. Davis served as commander of the 332nd Fighter Group in Italy during World War II.

EXTRA! EXTRA!

Flyboys Say, "Sky's the Limit!"

IMAGINE wanting to become a pilot more than anything. Now imagine someone saying you aren't allowed to fly because of the color of your skin. Many African Americans who dreamed of flying in the early days of airplanes faced segregation and discrimination on the airfield. Most flight training schools in the United States refused to train black pilots. Black pilots and their supporters worked tirelessly for years to gain access to the sky.

The same was true in the United States military. African American soldiers were treated differently. They were given far fewer opportunities to develop and use their skills while serving their country.

In December 1941, the United States entered World War II. Once again, African Americans in the military were kept separate from their white peers. Many military jobs—including flying military aircraft—were closed to them simply because of the color of their skin.

This situation was about to change, however. In 1941, the Army Air Corps reluctantly agreed to the "Tuskegee Experiment." On the grounds of the Tuskegee Institute in Tuskegee, Alabama, over 10,000 African Americans trained as pilots, navigators, airplane mechanics, and maintenance and support crews. This pioneering group of African American military aviators and crew members became known as the Tuskegee Airmen.

In 1943, the Tuskegee Airmen were sent into battle in North Africa, the Mediterranean, and Italy. Under the command of Col. Benjamin O. Davis, the highly trained fighter pilots flew approximately 1,500 successful missions, helping the United States and its allies claim victory over their enemies in World War II.

The skill and bravery shown by the Tuskegee Airmen helped prove to the United States military that the color of one's skin did not mean a thing on the ground or in the sky. Finally, in 1948 President Truman signed an executive order officially ending segregation in th United States military.

BE A
FLIGHT
LEADER!
LEAD A DANGEROUS
WORLD WAR II
MISSION OVER ITALY
WITH THE 332ND
FIGHTER GROUP OF
TUSKEGEE AIRMEN

Members of the 332nd Fighter Group painted the tails of their airplanes red, earning them the nickname "Red Tails." You can see this feature in an oil painting by W. S. Phillips titiled *Two Down, One to Go*.

Keep us flying!

BUY WAR BONDS

Tuskegee Airman William Diez is featured in this World War II plea for Americans to buy war bonds.

Eleanor Roosevelt and "Chief" Anderson take a flight at the Tuskegee Institute in Alabama.

First Lady Says, "You Can Fly, All Right!"

ON THE morning of March 29, 1941, the First Lady of the United States, Eleanor Roosevelt, made an official visit to the Tuskegee Institute in Alabama. Mrs. Roosevelt, as well as a crowd of reporters, was interested in learning more about the school's pilot training program for African Americans.

The First Lady's special visit was going along as planned until Mrs. Roosevelt requested a ride in an airplane with one of the school's African American pilots, "Chief" Anderson. Her shocked Secret Service men tried hard to stop her, even calling the president on a portable telephone. But as her husband, President Roosevelt, said, "If my wife has made up her mind to take a plane ride, I can't stop her."

According to Chief Anderson, "She told me, 'I always heard Negroes couldn't fly and I wondered if you'd mind taking me up.' All her escorts got tremendously upset and told her she shouldn't do it."

Soon, Anderson and the First Lady were strapped inside the two-seater Piper J-3 airplane. Anderson was cleared for takeoff, and the airplane flew off into the Alabama sky.

The crowd on the ground watched the airplane disappear over the countryside, and waited anxiously for its return. Finally, the small airplane dropped from the clouds and came in for a flawless landing.

"When we came back, she said, 'Well, you can fly all right.' I'm positive that when she went home, she said, 'Franklin, I flew with those boys down there, and you're going to have to do something about it,'" reported Anderson.

Without a doubt, the First Lady made a big statement with her exciting flight above the Tuskegee Institute. Her determination to fly showed the world her unquestionable confidence and support of the African American pilots, known as the Tuskegee Airmen.

operations; it's up high so everything can be seen on deck and out at sea

pri-fly—short for "primary flight control"; located on the island, this is where all flight operations are controlled

air boss—the captain in charge of the entire aircraft carrier

mini-boss—the air boss' assistant

helmsman—the person who steers the aircraft carrier and controls the speed of the ship

elevator—for lifting jets from the hangar deck (down below) to the flight deck

arresting wire—strong cables that hook onto a jet to help slow it down quickly

Landing a jet on a moving runway in the middle of the ocean leaves little room for error.

SEE IF YOU CAN SPOT:
✓ CHECK THE ONES YOU FIND

☐ 4 aircraft elevators

☐ folded wings

☐ 2 rudders

☐ jet blast deflectors

☐ the air search radar

☐ the squadron ready room

MEET A NAVY FIGHTER PILOT

HI! I'M LIEUTENANT COMMANDER KEVIN CHLAN, OF THE UNITED STATES NAVY. I GRADUATED FROM THE UNITED STATES NAVAL ACADEMY IN ANNAPOLIS, MARYLAND. I HAVE BEEN FLYING JETS SINCE 2000. I FLY THE F/A-18E/F SUPER HORNET.

Would you be brave enough to land an F-18 Super Hornet on an aircraft carrier? Lieutenant Commander Kevin Chlan does it for a living!

What were you like as a kid?

I was interested in sports (baseball, volleyball, football) and music. Music has really continued to be a lifelong passion of mine. In school, I was always interested in math and science.

When did you know you wanted to be a pilot?

On the first day of school at the Naval Academy, two F-14 Tomcats flew over us, and it was one of the coolest things I had ever seen. By the time I was a senior at the Academy, I was certain that I wanted to become a naval aviator. I haven't regretted that decision a single day since then.

What do you do as a Navy pilot?

I have spent a lot of time deployed at sea, either on the USS *Kitty Hawk* or USS *Enterprise*. We fly a lot, both day and night. Our primary mission is to support American and coalition troops who are on the ground in harm's way.

How hard is it to fly an F-18 Super Hornet?

It's really not that hard, but it takes lots of training and practice! The jet actually flies very easily. Managing the weapons and all the systems is the part that takes lots of training.

What is it like to take off and land on an aircraft carrier?

Taking off from an aircraft carrier is actually very simple for the pilot, but it is quite a rush. You go from 0 to 130 miles per hour in about two seconds. Landing during the daytime is a lot of fun. It requires an awful lot of practice and skill. You are trying to line up and catch one of four wires on a runway that is moving away from you, and also moving sideways. In order to "catch a wire," you need to land at precisely the right location, at the right airspeed, with the right rate of descent. Every time you touch down, you have to select full power just in case the wire doesn't catch and you have to go flying again (which is called a "bolter"). I have had about 550 carrier landings in my career (some of them better than others!). Landing at night is a different story. I probably have had about 250 night landings, and my legs still shake with fear every single time I come aboard at night.

What are the best parts of being on an aircraft carrier? What are the biggest challenges?

Getting to fly off the ship is always the best part of the day. Being away from my family is, by far, the biggest challenge.

HOW THINGS FLY IN SPACE

I'M ANDREW. I'M AN EXPLAINER HERE AT THE MUSEUM. LET ME EXPLAIN SOME OF THE FASCINATING FACTS ABOUT GETTING TO AND MOVING AROUND IN SPACE.

COMPARISON CHART
IF YOU WEIGH 70 POUNDS HERE ON EARTH, YOU WOULD WEIGH:

About 26 pounds on Mercury

About 63 pounds on Venus

70 POUNDS ON EARTH

About 12 pounds on Moon

About 26 pounds on Mars

About 165 pounds on Jupiter

About 74 pounds on Saturn

About 62 pounds on Uranus

About 79 pounds on Neptune

About 5 pounds on Pluto

AND, ABOUT 1,895 POUNDS ON THE SUN!

Beyond Earth's atmosphere, only two forces affect flight: weight and thrust. In the vacuum of space, there is no air. Without air there is no air pressure to create lift and there are no air molecules to cause drag.

Weight

Are you weightless in space? Not really. Weight is the force of gravity acting on the mass of an object. Although we talk about astronauts experiencing weightlessness, objects in space have mass and the force of gravity affects them. In fact, gravity is what holds a spacecraft in orbit. Without gravity, the spacecraft would fly off in a straight line.

If gravity is pulling on an orbiting spacecraft, why doesn't it fall to Earth? The spacecraft is falling, but it is moving forward as fast as it is falling. The path of an orbiting spacecraft matches the curve of the Earth. Even before space travel, Isaac Newton imagined shooting a cannon ball from a mountain fast enough for it to move beyond the Earth before it fell to Earth.

CHECK IT OUT!
TRY OUT NEWTON'S CANNON AND LEARN WHY YOU ARE NOT REALLY WEIGHTLESS IN SPACE.

ASTRONAUT

6 feet
1.5 meters

34 feet
10.4 meters

COMMAND AND SERVICE MODULE

SATURN V

363 feet/111 meters

CAN YOU FIND THIS?
SEE IF YOU CAN FIND THE THRUSTERS ON THE APOLLO 11 COMMAND MODULE, *COLUMBIA,* LOCATED IN *MILESTONES OF FLIGHT* (GALLERY 100), OR ONLINE.

Thrust

Spacecraft use rocket engines to create thrust. By firing a thruster in one direction, a spacecraft will move in the opposite direction. To rotate, the spacecraft fires a pair of thrusters located on the sides of the spacecraft. To stop rotating, the spacecraft fires a pair of thrusters aimed in the opposite direction.

Thrusters can be used to change speed. When traveling through space, a spacecraft fires rear-facing thrusters to speed up and forward-facing thrusters to slow down. When in orbit, things are different. To speed up while in orbit, the spacecraft fires a thruster in the forward direction. This drops it into a lower orbit, and increases its speed. To slow down, the spacecraft fires a thruster in the rear direction. This pushes it into a higher orbit, and slows it down.

Spacecraft sometimes use gyroscopes to maneuver. A gyroscope is a device with heavy wheels that spin very fast. If there is a small push on the gyroscope in one direction, it will resist and push the spacecraft in the other direction.

How do rocket engines work? Unlike jet engines, rocket engines don't need air. There is an oxidizer inside the rocket engine that helps fuel burn. When the oxidizer and fuel are ignited, the engine produces thrust. With no drag to slow it down, the spacecraft will keep moving in the same direction.

The Saturn V rocket was used to send astronauts to the moon.

Do you **SEE HOW SMALL THE COMMAND MODULE AND ASTRONAUTS ARE** compared to the rocket? That's because it requires that much power to send even small objects into space!

The Saturn V rocket was packed with fuel and engines that created awesome thrust to push the Apollo spacecraft into space. In fact, when it was full of fuel it weighed more than about 400 elephants and held enough fuel for a car to drive around the world 800 times!

TAKE A LOOK!
SEE A FOUR-FOOT-HIGH MODEL OF THE SATURN V ROCKET IN THE JAMES S. MCDONNELL SPACE HANGAR AT THE NATIONAL AIR AND SPACE MUSEUM'S STEVEN F. UDVAR-HAZY CENTER, OR ONLINE.

Other than orbiting Earth, Sputnik didn't do much, but it got a lot of attention for being the world's first satellite. **THE SPACE RACE WAS ON,** and within months the United States responded by launching its first satellite, called Explorer 1. It rocketed into orbit on January 31, 1958. Who would be the first to send a person into space? Who would be the first to land on the moon? These were questions kids, adults, scientists, and politicians were racing to answer.

Sputnik's long antennae transmitted a radio signal detected on Earth by scientists and amateur radio operators.

WHAT IS A SATELLITE?
IT'S AN OBJECT THAT ORBITS A LARGER OBJECT. IT CAN BE MAN-MADE, LIKE *SPUTNIK* AND *EXPLORER 1,* OR NATURAL, LIKE THE MOON.

Orbiting Earth for 105 days, Explorer 1 collected information on cosmic radiation and micrometeorites.

LOOK UP!

WANT TO KNOW MORE?
FIND MORE DETAILS ABOUT *SPUTNIK* AND *EXPLORER 1* ONLINE.

Can you spot Sputnik?

What three words would you use to describe Sputnik?

....

Now, look for Explorer 1.

What words would you use to describe Explorer 1?

....

Why do you think these two satellites look so different?

....

HUMANS IN SPACE? LET'S TRY ANIMALS FIRST

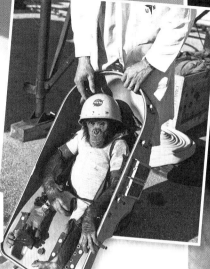

Ham took a 17-minute ride into space aboard the Mercury 5 spacecraft.

After the launch of Sputnik and Explorer 1, the big question on everyone's mind was, **"CAN WE SEND PEOPLE INTO SPACE?"**

A lot of questions needed to be answered first. Since no human had ever been to space, there was no telling what the journey would be like and what effect it could have on the human body. Scientists were particularly concerned about the effects of weightlessness on a person.

One way scientists could answer these questions was by sending animals into space. Insects, mice, dogs, and monkeys were among the first living creatures to take flight into space. Their successful (and sometimes unsuccessful) journeys helped scientists understand what needed to be done to keep future astronauts safe in space.

Meet some animal space travelers

Laika, a stray dog from Moscow, was launched into orbit by the Russians aboard Sputnik 2 in 1957. She earned the nickname "Muttnik."

HAM, the first chimpanzee space traveler in 1961, paved the way for the first American human in space, Alan Shepard.

ANITA and **ARABELLA** were spiders who flew aboard Skylab for 59 days in 1973. Astronauts watched to see if the spiders could spin webs in space. They could—after a little practice in their weightless environment! The experiment was designed by Judy Miles, a high school student from Massachusetts.

ABLE, a rhesus monkey, and **BAKER**, a squirrel monkey, traveled 360 miles into space in 1959 on an American rocket. They were the first animals to return safely to Earth after traveling to space.

CHECK ALL OF THE ANIMALS BELOW THAT YOU THINK HAVE TRAVELED IN SPACE.

- [ ] monkeys
- [ ] mice
- [ ] dogs
- [ ] rabbits
- [ ] fruit flies
- [ ] guinea pigs
- [ ] chimpanzees
- [ ] cats
- [ ] mealworms
- [ ] turtles
- [ ] spiders
- [ ] fish
- [ ] jellyfish
- [ ] rats
- [ ] bees
- [ ] tortoises
- [ ] newts
- [ ] frogs
- [ ] ants
- [ ] earthworms

Baker sits on a model of the Jupiter Missile that carried her into space.

TAKE A LOOK! YOU CAN SEE ANITA ON DISPLAY AT THE STEVEN F. UDVAR-HAZY CENTER IN THE *SPACE SCIENCE* EXHIBIT.

ANITA

Able is laying in her traveling "couch." See Able in *Apollo to the Moon* (Gallery 210).

Did you check them all? You should have, because they have all been to space! In fact, many more animals than people have flown in space.

27

Alan Shepard is being hoisted onto a US Marine helicopter after splashing down into the ocean in his *Freedom 7* capsule.

Edward White on (Extravehicular A or space walk, tethered to Gem

EXPLORATION BY THE UNITED STATES

CHECK IT OUT!
READ ABOUT OTHER APOLLO MISSIONS. SEE IF YOU CAN FIND OUT WHICH ASTRONAUT WAS THE LAST TO WALK ON THE MOON.

Neil Armstrong took this picture of Buzz Aldrin walking on the moon. What can you see in the reflection on his helmet?

Apollo Program

GOALS:

- Improve space exploration technology
- Be the first country to land humans on the moon
- Conduct scientific exploration of the moon
- Learn how to work on the moon

DID YOU KNOW?
THE FIRST HUMAN IN SPACE WAS SOVIET COSMONAUT YURI GAGARIN. ON APRIL 12, 1961 HIS ONE-ORBIT MISSION IN VOSTOK 1 LASTED 108 MINUTES.

DECEMBER 21–27, 1968

JULY 16–24, 1969

DECEMBER 7–19, 1972

Apollo 8

Apollo 8 astronauts, Frank Borman, James Lovell, and William Anders became the first astronauts to orbit the Moon, and spent Christmas Eve in orbit there.

This famous photograph of Earth was taken by Apollo 8 astronauts while they flew past the moon. Apollo astronauts were the first humans to photograph Earth while orbiting the moon.

Apollo 11

Apollo 11 astronauts Neil Armstrong and Edwin (Buzz) Aldrin successfully landed the lunar module on the Moon and were the first astronauts to walk on the Moon. Command module pilot Michael Collins stayed with the command module in space.

Apollo 17

Apollo 17 was the sixth and last Apollo mission to land astronauts on the Moon. Mission commander Eugene "Gene" Cernan holds the distinction of being the last man to walk on the Moon, as no humans have visited since he stepped off the surface on December 14, 1972. The Apollo 17 lunar module also carried the only trained geologist to walk on the lunar surface, Harrison "Jack" Schmitt. Ronald Evans, the third Apollo 17 astronaut, remained in orbit around the Moon. Compared to previous Apollo missions, Apollo 17 astronauts traversed the greatest distance using the Lunar Roving Vehicle and returned the greatest amount of rock and soil samples.

KNOW THE LINGO!

rendezvous—bringing two spacecraft close together in space; requires very precise piloting

docking—joining two spacecraft together in space

Voyager—In 1979, two Voyager space probes were launched into the solar system. they sent back a great amount of information about the planets. They continue to travel beyond the solar system and are still transmitting information to scientists on Earth.

Find it in *Exploring the Planets* (Gallery 207).

Lunar Orbiter—this is an example of one of five robotic spacecraft that helped map the moon in the 1960s in preparation for the Apollo astronauts' arrival.

Find it in *Lunar Exploration Vehicles* (Gallery 112).

SPACECRAFT: A GREAT IDEA!

Why robotic spacecraft?

Robotic spacecraft aren't as particular as **HUMAN SPACE EXPLORERS**. They don't need food or water; they don't need air or a spacesuit; they don't need to go to the bathroom; and they don't need friends to keep them company. Also, they do what they are asked to do without grumbling—give them instructions, and off they go. However, they aren't perfect. Sometimes they break down, make mistakes, or don't respond to commands.

Space traveling humans have only set foot on the moon. Robotic spacecraft have been able to **GET UP CLOSE AND PERSONAL** with planets, moons, and other objects in our solar system. They have landed on the Moon, Venus, and Mars, and even on an asteroid and a moon of Saturn. They have taken close-up photographs of all of the planets and even collected dust from the tail of a comet. Many are **ZOOMING THROUGH SPACE** this very minute. They are flying by distant planets and moons, collecting information for curious scientists waiting to study it in the comfort of their labs here on Earth.

Robotic spacecraft take a lot of **HUMAN BRAINPOWER** and money to make, and they are only as smart as the humans who make them. They don't have brains like us, and can't think on their own. But, they are able to **GO WHERE HUMANS CANNOT GO**. If something goes wrong there are no human lives at stake.

Lander

A robotic spacecraft that lands or crashes into the surface of a planet or moon to collect information, and stays where it lands

Viking lander—two Viking landers were the first robotic spacecraft to land successfully on the surface of Mars.

Find it in *Milestones of Flight* (Gallery 100).

Rover

Like a lander, but capable of moving around on the surface of a planet or moon

What big differences can you spot on these four robotic spacecraft?

Mars Exploration Rover—two rovers were launched in 2003 to explore the surface of Mars. These "robotic geologists" were built to last 90 days, but they both operated for several years studying the rocks and soil on Mars.

Find it in *Exploring the Planets* (Gallery 207).

Alan Bean began his career as a navy pilot.

MEET APOLLO ASTRONAUT

It is hard to imagine what it would be like to walk on another world in space. Would it be scary? Exciting? Lonely? Peaceful? Amazing? The first people to set foot on the Moon were Apollo 11 astronauts Neil Armstrong and Buzz Aldrin. Michael Collins, the third astronaut on the trip, stayed in lunar orbit in the command module. You can find out more about this journey in *Apollo to the Moon* (Gallery 210).

In November 1969, **ALAN BEAN** and his crewmates Pete Conrad and Richard Gordon flew to the moon in a spacecraft called the *YANKEE CLIPPER*. Captain Bean was one of only 12 people to walk on the moon. A few years later, in 1973, Captain Bean was the commander of **SKYLAB**, the United States' first space station. He stayed on Skylab for 59 days.

Here is a behind-the-scenes interview with a true explorer, or, as Captain Bean says, one lucky guy!

What is it that made you want to be an astronaut?

Flying in rocket ships and going to another world seemed like the most fun thing that anyone could do!

How long does it take to become an astronaut?

Before you can be an astronaut, you have to have a lot of skills, whether it's flying airplanes (that was the skill I had), or being a geologist, or meteorologist, or a doctor. So it takes maybe 10 years after you graduate from college to get good enough to be selected as an astronaut. Then it takes another three or so years to learn the astronaut things.

What did your first spaceflight feel like?

It felt wonderful! The sights were amazing. It was a little bit scary, but it was worth it. A lot of things that are a little scary are worth it.

Captain Alan Bean, seen here in his spacesuit, was the fourth person to set foot on the moon. He considers himself one of the luckiest people on Earth.

AND ARTIST ALAN BEAN

Captain Bean spent 59 days orbiting Earth on Skylab.

Does it stink in your space gear?

No, your space gear is very, very clean and you keep it that way because you want it to operate properly.

Were there any scary moments on the Apollo 12 mission?

We were struck by lightning. We never expected that! But with the help of Mission Control, we worked together as a team and solved the problems.

What is it like looking back at Earth?

Earth looks amazingly small. It is very beautiful. It looks like a small blue-and-white marble. It looks very shiny. When you look at the Moon from Earth, it's not always full. That's exactly how it is when you look back at Earth from space. When we went to the Moon, Earth looked pretty full—about three quarters full. But when we came home 10 days later, we couldn't see very much of Earth.

Was it hard to walk on the moon? If you fall down, is it hard to get up?

It wasn't hard to walk on the Moon. You had to be careful of the rocks and little craters so you didn't step on something and turn your ankle. If you fell down—which I did a couple times—it wasn't hard to get up because you weigh only one-sixth of what you weigh on Earth. But it takes a lot of energy, so it's better if your teammate comes over and lifts you up.

Do you view yourself as a great explorer?

No. I view myself as a lucky person, one of the luckiest people on Earth who got a chance to take part in a great exploration. I was a regular person, and NASA turned me into an explorer.

What are your thoughts on the future of space exploration?

Space is an ocean whose farthest shore we can never reach. So, no matter how much exploration we do now, there will always be more to do. There are so many great adventures awaiting future generations!

You are an exceptional and unique artist. Why did you decide to devote yourself to making art?

Twelve people walked on the Moon, and we were lucky to get the opportunity to do it. I realized this was one of the great explorations in all history, one of the great adventures. I thought, I can paint some of these adventures that we all had in this Apollo program, so that when we're gone, people can look at my paintings and be inspired to take the next step. I decided to become an artist so that I can celebrate this great adventure and pass it on.

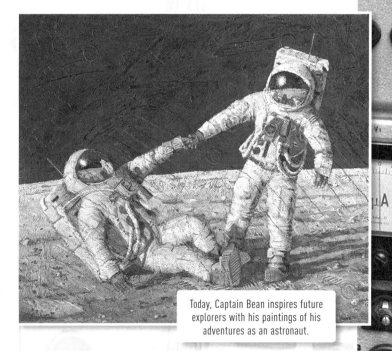

Today, Captain Bean inspires future explorers with his paintings of his adventures as an astronaut.

CAN YOU SPOT THESE SKYLAB FEATURES?

✓ CHECK THE ONES YOU FIND

☐ Three bedrooms (Shhh... someone is sleeping in one.)

☐ Toilet with handles (Better hold on since there's no gravity to keep you seated. This toilet is on the wall!)

☐ A paper Christmas tree (Astronauts were in Skylab during the holidays in 1973.)

☐ Shower (This turned out to be complicated because it took over 45 minutes to shower in space, and all of the water had to be wiped and vacuumed up so the water drops wouldn't float around the lab!)

☐ Snoopy! (Red, white, and blue Snoopy stickers marked the belongings of different crew members.)

☐ An exercise bicycle (Riding the bike for 90 minutes took an astronaut all the way around the world, since it took 90 minute to complete one orbit around Earth!)

INTERNATIONAL SPACE STATION

Today, we have the International Space Station (ISS), a group project of many nations!

Just hangin' around in zero gravity!

The ISS measures 357 feet from end to end and weighs almost one million pounds!

Astronaut Sandra Magnus dodges floating storage containers aboard the ISS.

ISS Fast Facts:

1. The ISS was created by the space agencies of the United States, Russia, Canada, Japan, and the countries of Europe.

2. It has been inhabited by humans since November 2, 2000.

3. Over 200 people have lived and worked on the ISS.

4. It was built in pieces, or modules, the first of which was the Russian module Zarya.

5. Including its large solar panels, it is the size of a football field (end zones included)!

6. The living area is about the size of a five-bedroom home, and includes two bathrooms and exercise equipment for working out.

7. It has a 55-foot robotic arm called Canadarm 2 that can move like an inchworm around the outside of the space station.

8. It includes three well-equipped science laboratories where astronauts conduct research on a daily basis.

Sandra Magnus' Journal
Living in Space

Imagine living in a place where you can never set anything down. If you set it down, it floats away and disappears. Nothing is stable. Take any activity that you do throughout the day and think about how much you rely on setting things down. In the morning, you get out of bed. Your bed is sitting on the floor, held there by gravity. You go to your drawer to get out your clothes. Your clothes are being held down in the drawer because of gravity. You take off your pj's and throw them on the floor, the bed, or in the clothes hamper. They stay put because of gravity. You get the idea. As you continue to think about your day, you will realize how much you take advantage of gravity. In our world up here on ISS we do not have that advantage.

I get up in the morning out of a sleeping bag that is tied to the wall. I open my container to get my clothes and they all want to float out. I can use friction as a force in my favor, by packing the clothes in tight, but when I take something out, that loosens up the whole stack and away they go. When I take off my pj's they float around in the crew quarters until I gather them up and immediately fasten them down behind a band or something. It is easy to lose things up here! That is why Velcro is our friend.

—Sandra Magnus

THE SPACE SHUTTLE ERA

After the success of the **MERCURY**, **GEMINI**, and **APOLLO** space programs of the 1960s and 1970s, the United States developed the Space Shuttle program, launching the world's first reusable spacecraft into Earth's orbit in 1981. Over the next 30 years, a total of **135 SPACE SHUTTLE MISSIONS** were launched.

The missions often involved delivering communications or scientific satellites into orbit, such as the Hubble Space Telescope, and conducting research experiments in space. Missions also included delivering and constructing parts of the International Space Station. The Space Shuttle program sent more than **350 ASTRONAUTS** to establish an orbital home and workplace, advancing toward the goal of a permanent human presence in space.

Space shuttle *Atlantis* rockets toward space.

Atlantis

CHECK IT OUT!
GET AN INSIDE-LOOK AT THE *DISCOVERY* FLIGHT DECK, MID-DECK (CREW QUARTERS), AND PAYLOAD AREA.

The Space Shuttle Program by the Numbers:

30 YEARS of space missions, from April 1981 to July 2011

135 space shuttle launches

5 SPACE SHUTTLE ORBITERS: *Columbia, Challenger, Discovery, Atlantis,* and *Endeavour*

1 SPACE SHUTTLE TEST VEHICLE: *Enterprise*

3 MAIN PARTS of the space shuttle: large fuel tank, pair of long white rocket boosters, orbiter vehicle, which carries the astronauts and payload (cargo) into space

60-FOOT-LONG PAYLOAD compartment on the orbiter is used for carrying satellites, supplies, and other cargo into space.

122 FEET from orbiter's nose to tail

78-FOOT WINGSPAN

4,500,000 POUNDS LIFTOFF WEIGHT of the "stack" includes the orbiter, two rocket boosters, and the full fuel tank (plus more, depending on what the shuttle is carrying).

17,500 MILES PER HOUR orbiting speed

355 ASTRONAUTS flew on missions, most more than once; 49 of these astronauts were women.

2 SHUTTLES LOST—*Challenger* was lost in an accident during launch on January 28, 1986; *Columbia* was lost in an accident upon re-entry into Earth's atmosphere on February 1, 2003.

14 ASTRONAUTS were lost in the two space shuttle accidents.

2 ASTRONAUTS were on the smallest crew.

8 ASTRONAUTS were on the largest crew.

77 YEARS OLD—The oldest astronaut in space, John Glenn, flew on *Discovery* in 1998.

28 YEARS OLD—The youngest astronaut in space, Sultan bin Salman bin Abdul-Aziz Al Saud (who happened to be a prince from Saudi Arabia), flew on *Discovery* in 1985.

537.1 MILLION MILES traveled by the space shuttles

1,334 DAYS spent in space by shuttle orbiters

THE SPACESUIT

DRAW YOUR SPACESUIT DESIGN HERE

We are pretty lucky to live here on planet Earth, with its **"JUST-RIGHT" ENVIRONMENT**. We have air to breathe, protection from much of the sun's intense light, and the right balance of air pressure to **STAY COMFORTABLE**. If we want to go outside, we just walk out the door. Yes, sometimes we have to put on a jacket to keep warm, but overall, it doesn't take much preparation for us to go about our daily lives here on Earth.

Living in space is a **COMPLETELY DIFFERENT** matter. If an astronaut decided to take a stroll outside the controlled environment of the spacecraft, he or she wouldn't last a minute. With no air, no air pressure, and extremely low temperatures in space, the astronaut would faint, swell up, and start to freeze within seconds. With **NO PROTECTION** from the sun's rays, the astronaut would quickly get a bad sunburn. Death would be certain.

That is why you always see astronauts in spacesuits when they are outside of their spacecraft. A spacesuit is an astronaut's own **PRIVATE SPACECRAFT**, or **SURVIVAL SUIT**. During the Space Shuttle era its official name was an extravehicular mobility unit (unofficially: an out-of-the-spacecraft-moving-around-survival-suit). A spacesuit makes life in space possible by providing warmth, air to breathe, pressure to keep the body functioning properly, and protection from the sun.

KNOW THE LINGO!

EVA (Extravehicular activity)—a space walk; spacesuits are required!

SAFER—(Simplified Aid For EVA Rescue) a small jet-pack that would help an astronaut get back to the spacecraft if he or she became un-tethered and drifted off.

MAG (Maximum Absorption Garment)— you guessed it, this is an adult-size diaper for long spacewalks (unseen).

The spacesuit is an astronaut's personal survival system in space.

DID YOU KNOW? IT TAKES ABOUT 45 MINUTES TO PUT ON A SPACESUIT. PUTTING IT ON IS CALLED "DONNING". TAKING IT OFF IS CALLED "DOFFING".

HOW WELL DO YOU KNOW YOUR SOLAR SYSTEM?

TRY THIS AT HOME!

WHAT'S WHAT in the solar system? **TEST YOUR KNOWLEDGE** by matching the clues with the planets of the solar system.

CHECK IT OUT! FOR MORE SOLAR SYSTEM FACTS, VISIT *EXPLORING THE PLANETS* (GALLERY 207).

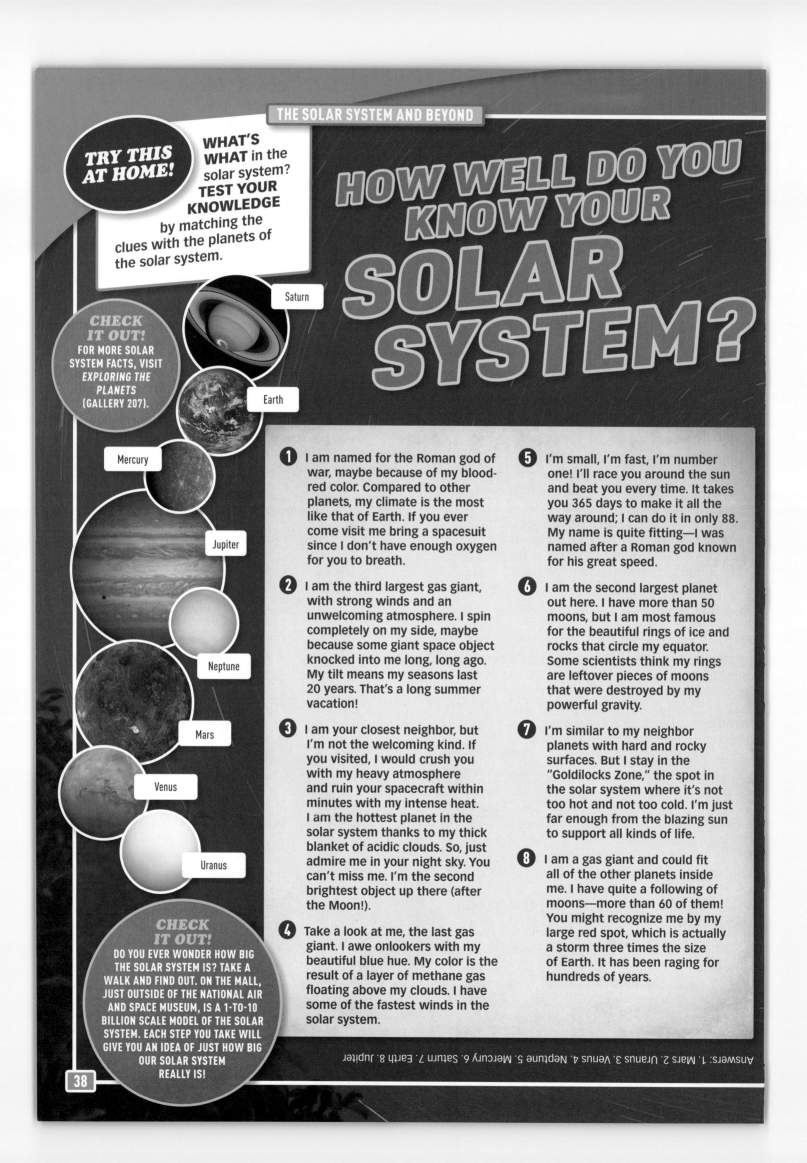

Saturn

Earth

Mercury

Jupiter

Neptune

Mars

Venus

Uranus

CHECK IT OUT! DO YOU EVER WONDER HOW BIG THE SOLAR SYSTEM IS? TAKE A WALK AND FIND OUT. ON THE MALL, JUST OUTSIDE OF THE NATIONAL AIR AND SPACE MUSEUM, IS A 1-TO-10 BILLION SCALE MODEL OF THE SOLAR SYSTEM. EACH STEP YOU TAKE WILL GIVE YOU AN IDEA OF JUST HOW BIG OUR SOLAR SYSTEM REALLY IS!

1 I am named for the Roman god of war, maybe because of my blood-red color. Compared to other planets, my climate is the most like that of Earth. If you ever come visit me bring a spacesuit since I don't have enough oxygen for you to breath.

2 I am the third largest gas giant, with strong winds and an unwelcoming atmosphere. I spin completely on my side, maybe because some giant space object knocked into me long, long ago. My tilt means my seasons last 20 years. That's a long summer vacation!

3 I am your closest neighbor, but I'm not the welcoming kind. If you visited, I would crush you with my heavy atmosphere and ruin your spacecraft within minutes with my intense heat. I am the hottest planet in the solar system thanks to my thick blanket of acidic clouds. So, just admire me in your night sky. You can't miss me. I'm the second brightest object up there (after the Moon!).

4 Take a look at me, the last gas giant. I awe onlookers with my beautiful blue hue. My color is the result of a layer of methane gas floating above my clouds. I have some of the fastest winds in the solar system.

5 I'm small, I'm fast, I'm number one! I'll race you around the sun and beat you every time. It takes you 365 days to make it all the way around; I can do it in only 88. My name is quite fitting—I was named after a Roman god known for his great speed.

6 I am the second largest planet out here. I have more than 50 moons, but I am most famous for the beautiful rings of ice and rocks that circle my equator. Some scientists think my rings are leftover pieces of moons that were destroyed by my powerful gravity.

7 I'm similar to my neighbor planets with hard and rocky surfaces. But I stay in the "Goldilocks Zone," the spot in the solar system where it's not too hot and not too cold. I'm just far enough from the blazing sun to support all kinds of life.

8 I am a gas giant and could fit all of the other planets inside me. I have quite a following of moons—more than 60 of them! You might recognize me by my large red spot, which is actually a storm three times the size of Earth. It has been raging for hundreds of years.

Answers: 1. Mars 2. Uranus 3. Venus 4. Neptune 5. Mercury 6. Saturn 7. Earth 8. Jupiter

POSTCARDS FROM BEYOND
VISIONS FROM THE HUBBLE SPACE TELESCOPE

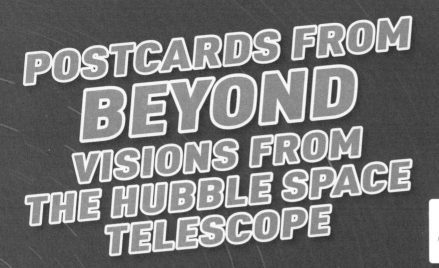

The Hubble Space Telescope has allowed earthlings to peer into the depths of space.

Have you ever looked at the night sky through a telescope? For centuries, curious astronomers have used telescopes to gaze deeper and deeper into space. Telescopes have come a long way since the first telescopes of hundreds of years ago. People are always trying to make them better, so they can see farther into the universe.

On April 24, 1990, the most advanced and powerful telescope ever made to examine the universe from space—the HUBBLE SPACE TELESCOPE—was launched. The bus-sized telescope was carried in the cargo hold of the space shuttle *Discovery*. It was released into its orbit 353 MILES ABOVE EARTH'S SURFACE. Traveling at a speed of 17,500 miles per hour, the telescope circles Earth every 97 minutes!

For more than 20 years, the Hubble Space Telescope has been busy taking images of planets in our solar system, never-before-seen stars, galaxies, and nebulae. Built with the most precise scientific instruments, it focuses its sight on OBJECTS DEEP IN SPACE. Its eight-foot-wide mirror collects more than 160,000 times the amount of light our eyes can ever detect, which enables it to image and electronically record galaxies MILLIONS OF LIGHT-YEARS AWAY!

Each week, the Hubble Space Telescope sends back 120 GIGABYTES OF DATA. That's about the same amount of information contained in 41,000 digital photos, 527,000 books, or 12 million emails! This information is studied by astronomers all over the world. Images from Hubble have helped scientists understand more about how the universe formed, including how stars and galaxies form and function.

Be sure to check out the HUBBLE TEST TELESCOPE in *Space Race* (Gallery 114). Astronauts once practiced their repair tasks on this telescope here on Earth before heading up to fix the real thing. Also, check out the back-up Hubble mirror in *Explore the Universe* (Gallery 111).

The Helix Nebula

DID YOU KNOW?
MANY PEOPLE THINK THIS DYING STAR, LOCATED IN THE CONSTELLATION AQUARIUS, LOOKS LIKE AN EYE. WHAT DO YOU THINK?

CHECK IT OUT!
MAKE YOUR OWN HAND-HELD HUBBLE TELESCOPE!

great collection of all things related to flight here on Earth and in space. **IT'S YOUR TURN TO DECIDE** which of the thousands of objects in the museum deserve special awards. **DRAW OR NAME** your favorite finds in the boxes on these pages.

JUDGE!

BEST AIRPLANE:

BEST SPACECRAFT:

OBJECT I WISH I COULD KEEP AS A SOUVENIER:

SpaceShipOne

MOST FASCINATING PILOT:

MOST AWESOME DESIGN:

Awesome!

MY FAVORITE
TALL OBJECT:

MOST
LIKELY TO
STICK IN MY MIND:

P-26A Peashooter

STRANGEST
FIND:

FASTEST
FLYING FIND:

ONE OF
MY OVERALL
FAVORITES:

BEST
SMALL OJECT:

I'LL TELL A
FRIEND ABOUT
THIS:

...take the elevator to the top of the Donald D. Engen Tower where you can observe planes taking off and landing nearby at Dulles International Airport.

...GARAGE OR SHED USED FOR STORING AIRPLANES OR SPACECRAFT.

...**WITH OVER 100 AIRPLANES AND 122 SPACE OBJECTS** to discover. Where will you begin?

CAN YOU FIND THESE AIRCRAFT WITH ANIMAL NAMES?

✓ **CHECK THE ONES YOU FIND**

- ☐ Eagle
- ☐ Hawk
- ☐ Albatross
- ☐ Sparrowhawk
- ☐ Falcon
- ☐ Bird Dog
- ☐ Bat
- ☐ Chipmunk
- ☐ Phoenix
- ☐ Viper
- ☐ Tomcat
- ☐ Bearcat
- ☐ Goose

- ☐ Hornet
- ☐ Katydid
- ☐ Blackbird
- ☐ Pterodactyl
- ☐ Mighty Mouse
- ☐ Mite
- ☐ Dragonfly
- ☐ Mustang
- ☐ Black Widow
- ☐ Scorpion
- ☐ Seahorse
- ☐ Kingfisher

MOBILE QUARANTINE FACILITY

No, this is not a shiny spacecraft—it's an Airstream trailer that the Apollo astronauts had to live in for a few days when they returned from the Moon. Why? Scientists thought they might have brought back moon germs! (Don't worry, they didn't.)

How would you like to spend almost three days stuck in a trailer after being in space for more than a week? What would you do for three days?

SO MUCH MORE TO SEE!

THE LOCKHEED SR-71 BLACKBIRD

JOURNAL

What do you notice about this plane, the SR-71 Blackbird?

This is the world's fastest airplane. Take a look at the shape of this plane. Its wings form a big triangle, or "delta," which helps it travel three times faster than the speed of sound!

AIR FRANCE

THE CONCORDE

Check out the shape of the Concorde. How is it similar to the Blackbird?

Need to get somewhere fast? This plane flew passengers at twice the speed of sound (Mach 2) from 1969 to 2003. It no longer flies because it is too expensive! The nose on the Concorde could be moved down to help the pilots see the runway when taking off and landing.

What is the most surprising thing about *Discovery*?

CHECK IT OUT!
WANT TO KNOW HOW THE SPACE SHUTTLE LIFTS OFF?

This is the orbiter portion of the space shuttle—the entire space shuttle included two rocket boosters and a huge fuel tank. *Discovery* made 39 flights into space, flying more astronauts and more miles than any other orbiter in the shuttle program.

United States

Discovery

SPACE SHUTTLE
DISCOVERY

National **AIR AND SPACE MUSEUM**. Then write a few lines to **YOURSELF** about your visit here! What do you want to **REMEMBER**?

LOOKING FOR MORE

The National Air and Space Museum

So, you think you've seen all there is to see at the National Air and Space Museum? Think again!

Space awaits your exploration!

CHECK IT OUT!
BE SURE TO CHECK OUT THE AWESOME ADVENTURES AT THE SMITHSONIAN: THE OFFICIAL KIDS GUIDE TO THE SMITHSONIAN WEBSITE. THE WEBSITE IS WHERE YOU CAN FIND LINKS TO ALL KINDS OF AT-HOME ACTIVITIES, RESOURCES, AND FUN BONUS MATERIAL.

Dear Me,

_____

_____

_____

_____

_____

Me!

My street!

My town!

My country!

Love, Me

AIR AND SPACE?

Don't miss your chance to touch a real moon rock!

THINK FAST!

20 QUESTIONS: After your visit to the National Air and Space Museum, answer these questions as fast as you can!

1. Was this your first time at the National Air and Space Museum? YES/NO

2. Did something amaze you? YES/NO

3. Did you learn something new? YES/NO

4. Did you go in the cockpit of the 747 jumbo jet? YES/NO

5. About how many people were at the museum today?

   ....

6. Do you want to learn how to fly? YES/NO

7. Would you like to be an astronaut someday? YES/NO

8. Would you volunteer to live on Mars? YES/NO

9. Did you go inside Skylab? YES/NO

10. Did you touch the moon rock? YES/NO

11. Did you see the space monkey, Able? YES/NO

12. Did you check out the lunar module? YES/NO

13. Did you walk through the DC-7? YES/NO

14. Did you watch an IMAX® movie? YES/NO

15. Did you see a planetarium show? YES/NO

16. Did you have fun? YES/NO

17. Did your legs get tired? YES/NO

18. Did you have some lunch? YES/NO

19. Are you still hungry? YES/NO

20. Where are you headed now?

   ....

The Age of Flight started with lots of experimentation with aircraft like this Wright glider. The experimentation continues today.

WHAT'S NEW?
MUSEUMS ARE CONSTANTLY CHANGING, KIND OF LIKE PEOPLE. IF YOU WANT TO KEEP UP WITH WHAT'S HAPPENING AT THE MUSEUM, HANG OUT AT THE NATIONAL AIR AND SPACE MUSEUM'S WEBSITE. IT WILL KEEP YOU POSTED ON EVERYTHING THAT IS HAPPENING AT THE NATIONAL AIR AND SPACE MUSEUM—ON THE MALL, AND AT THE STEVEN F. UDVAR-HAZY CENTER.

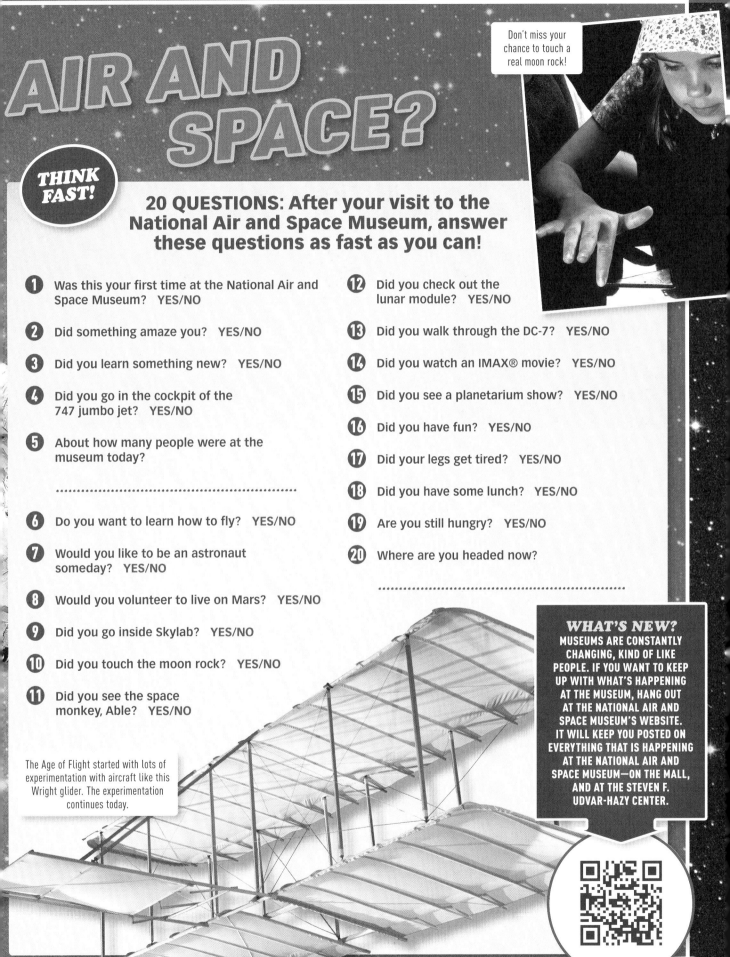

Buzz on by the *Insect Zoo* and watch some arthropods in action.

Your early ancestors await your visit.

This wild-looking octopus, featured in the *Sant Ocean Hall*, lives in the deepest, darkest parts of the ocean.

THINGS TO SEE AND DO AT THE NATIONAL MUSEUM OF NATURAL HISTORY:

- [ ] Stand next to an African elephant and discover the many creatures living alongside it in the Rotunda. Can you spot a vulture circling high above?
- [ ] Get up close and personal with fossils of some of the largest creatures that ever roamed the earth in the *Hall of Paleobiology*.
- [ ] Grab a seat in the Evolution Theater and watch a movie about your mammal relatives in the *Kenneth E. Behring Family Hall of Mammals*.
- [ ] Surround yourself with ocean life, including a life-sized model of a North Atlantic right whale, a preserved giant squid, and a live coral reef teeming with fish and other creatures in the *Sant Ocean Hall*.
- [ ] Wander among hundreds of butterflies fluttering through the Butterfly Pavilion. (Purchase tickets at the entrance.)
- [ ] Touch and observe live insects, and watch a live tarantula feeding at the *O. Orkin Insect Zoo*.
- [ ] Come face-to-face with amazing recreations of early humans in the *David H. Koch Hall of Human Origins*.
- [ ] Gawk at amazing gems and minerals, including the Hope Diamond, in the *Janet Annenberg Hooker Hall of Geology, Gems, and Minerals*.
- [ ] Touch meteorites that have traveled light-years through space in the *Meteorites and Solar System Gallery*.
- [ ] Touch everything in the Discovery Room—a room created just for kids!
- [ ] Browse through museum collections, talk with museum scientists, and use scientific tools in Q?RIUS, the education center.

WELCOME TO THE NATIONAL MUSEUM OF NATURAL HISTORY

Welcome to the wildest museum on the National Mall. This is the place to uncover the secrets of life here on Earth. Here at the **NATIONAL MUSEUM OF NATURAL HISTORY**, you can uncover the story of the world and all the life in it.

It's a bit overwhelming to think about, don't you think? How did Earth get here? Where did all this life come from? How did it develop and change over time? How did we get here? At the National Museum of Natural History, scientists try to answer these questions by studying scientific evidence.

What is this scientific evidence? Well, it's the 126 million objects in the National Museum of Natural History's collection! Each object in the museum's collection is a puzzle piece that helps us understand the natural world and our place in it.

For years and years, scientists, and people like you, have been collecting things found in the natural world. Here at the National Museum of Natural History, those items are carefully stored and studied by scientists from all over the world. Some of the collection even makes it into the exhibit halls for visitors like you to see. The great thing is this: the collecting will never end! About 750,000 items are added to the collection each year, along with new exhibitions.

NOW IT'S TIME FOR YOU TO BE THE SCIENTIST. As you explore the museum, get curious, ask questions, look carefully, collect information, and see what you can figure out about the world. **AND DON'T FORGET TO HAVE FUN!**

What's the story?

JOURNAL

What are you most excited to see at the National Museum of Natural History?

NATIONAL MUSEUM

Here are some of the fascinating finds you can discover at the National Museum of Natural History.

MAP KEY

- Security
- Accessibility
- Information Desk
- Information Kiosk
- Automated Teller
- Rest Rooms
- Museum Store
- Elevator
- Escalator
- Telephone
- Coat Room
- Stairs

GROUND FLOOR

Constitution Avenue Entrance

Atrium Café
(Elevator/ stairs to IMAX® Theater)

Museum Store

Museum Store

Museum Store

Birds of D.C.

Baird Auditorium

Birds of D.C.

Look up to see a live-size North Atlantic right whale.

HALL OF HUMAN ORIGINS

What do you know about your early human ancestors?

BIRDS OF DC

Can you find the yellow warbler among all of the other birds displayed?

HALL OF MAMMALS

There are 274 amazing animals hanging out here!

Investigate live insects, spiders, scorpions, centipedes, and more.

INSECT ZOO

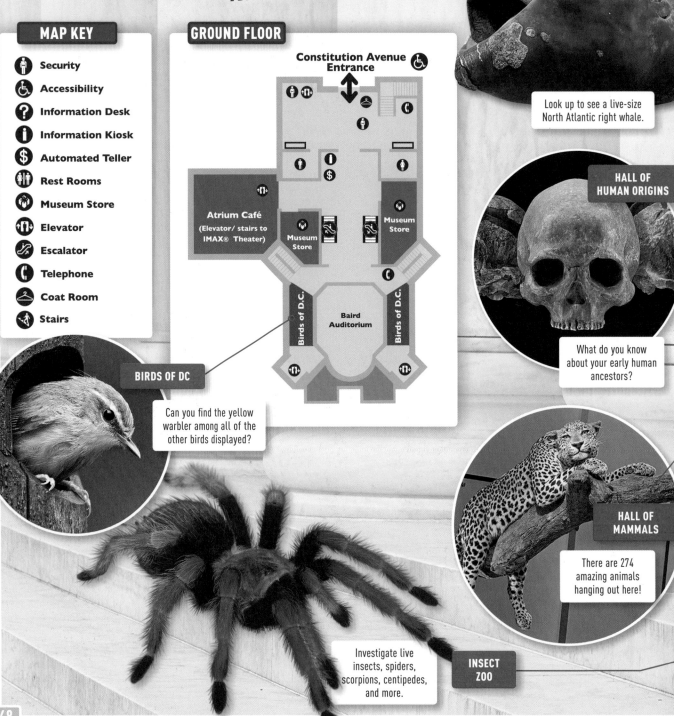

NATURAL HISTORY

FIRST FLOOR

OCEAN HALL

Human Origins

Ocean Hall

Special Exhibit Gallery

Special Exhibit Gallery

Discovery Room

African Cultures

ICE AGE

IMAX Theater Lobby

Ice Age

Check out fossilized remains of creatures large and small, like this Woolly Mammoth.

Special Exhibit Gallery

Ancient Seas

FossiLab

TTY

IMAX Tickets

Mammal Hall

Dinosaurs

Fossil Mammals

Rotunda

Early Life

Fossil Plants

Fossil Café

Mammals Store

An ever-changing selection of temporary exhibits—just ask the folks at the Information desk, "What's new?"

Mall Entrance

INFORMATION DESK

SECOND FLOOR

Korea Gallery

Take a look at massive meteorites and specks of space dust.

Written in Bone

IMAX Theater (EXIT)

Special Exhibit Gallery

Special Exhibit Gallery

HOPE DIAMOND

See the famous Hope Diamond, which never stops sparkling.

Egyptian Mummies

Bones

EARTH, MOON, AND METEORITES GALLERY

Insect Zoo

Hope Diamond

HALL OF GEOLOGY, GEMS, AND MINERALS

Butterflies + Plants

Geology, Gems & Minerals

Exhibits about volcanoes, earthquakes, and our ever-changing Earth.

Can a woolly mammoth frozen during an ice age be a fossil? Can hardened tree sap and the bugs caught inside be a fossil? Can dinosaur poop be a fossil? Yes, yes, and yes! Read this to figure out what is a fossil and what's not.

FOSSILS are more than just dinosaur bones! A fossil is any trace of life that is at least 10,000 years old. **BODY FOSSILS** are the remains of an animal. Fossils can also be the remains of a plant, bacteria, or fungus (fossilized mold, anyone?). They can even be things such as ancient footprints, animal tracks, burrows, and even dung (that's animal poop!). These kinds of fossils are called **TRACE FOSSILS** because they show us a trace of ancient life.

Sometimes body remains are preserved in a way that doesn't change them that much. For example, imagine a saber tooth tiger on the hunt 25,000 years ago. It tackles a horse, knocking both the horse and itself into a tar pit—never to escape. The animals are preserved in the tar pit for thousands of years until a **PALEONTOLOGIST** removes them from the pit. Only bones remain, but the bones have not changed. They are still made up of the same substances that they were made of when the animals were alive.

In other cases, the remains of living things are preserved but are chemically changed. These kinds of fossils tend to be much older. Imagine a *Stegosaurus* killed by a predator on the shores of a lake 150 million years ago. The soft parts of the dinosaur are eaten away by the predator and by bacteria. Most of the bones remain. The bones are quickly covered by **SEDIMENT**—that means dirt. Over time, the materials that make up the bones are gradually replaced by minerals found in the sediment around them. Over a long period of time, the bones are almost completely made up of the new minerals and are as hard as rock (because they are rock). The bones are now official fossils.

You may think that fossils are pretty common. We sure do have a lot of them in the museum! In reality, the chance of a living thing becoming a fossil is very small. The conditions required to make a fossil don't occur often and they only occur in certain environments, such as near the water. This means that almost all living things that have ever inhabited the earth leave no fossils or any other trace that they ever existed.

KNOW THE LINGO!

paleobiology—the study of ancient life

paleontologist—a scientist who studies ancient life by examining fossils

body fossil—the fossilized parts of an animal, like bones

trace fossil—fossilized signs of life, like footprints, nests, or burrows

coprolite—fossilized animal poop

sedimentary rock—rock that is made from compacted particles of sand, dirt, and the remains of plants and animals; fossils are found in sedimentary rock

TRY THIS AT HOME!

THINK LIKE A PALEONTOLOGIST. Take a look at the objects below. Are they fossils? How do you know? (Remember, **FOSSILS ARE THE REMAINS OF LIFE** more than 10,000 years old. They can be body fossils or trace fossils.) Now that **YOU KNOW ABOUT FOSSILS**, let's see if you can **IDENTIFY SOME**!

THIS IS A TRILOBITE THAT LIVED IN THE OCEAN OVER 250 MILLION YEARS AGO. IS IT A FOSSIL?

THIS IS A TOOTH FROM A *TYRANNOSAURUS REX*. IS IT A FOSSIL?

THIS IS AN ANCIENT ROMAN JUG. IS IT A FOSSIL?

THIS INSECT HAS BEEN PRESERVED IN AMBER (TREE SAP) FOR MILLIONS OF YEARS. IS IT A FOSSIL?

WHICH ARE FOSSILS?

CHECK OUT THIS DINOSAUR FOOTPRINT. IS IT A FOSSIL?

THIS PETRIFIED BACTERIA IS ABOUT 850 MILLION YEARS OLD! IS IT A FOSSIL?

THIS IS A DENDRITE STONE. THE FERN-LIKE PATTERN ON THE STONE IS MADE FROM MINERALS FLOWING THROUGH THE STONE. IS IT A FOSSIL?

THIS 40,000-YEAR-OLD, MUMMIFIED WOOLLY MAMMOTH BABY, NAMED LUBYA, WAS DISCOVERED IN RUSSIA IN 2007. IS IT A FOSSIL?

THIS IS *T. REX* POOP THAT HAS TURNED INTO STONE. IS IT A FOSSIL?

THIS IS PETRIFIED WOOD, AN ANCIENT TREE THAT HAS BECOME A ROCK. IS IT A FOSSIL?

Answers: Only two of these are not fossils. The pottery is an artifact—something made by people. Neither are fossils. The dendrite stone shows a naturally occurring pattern that forms on limestone rock. All of the other examples are fossils of living things. Can you tell which are body fossils and which are trace fossils?

PALEONTOLOGIST

Dr. Carrano is the Curator of Dinosauria at the Smithsonian's National Museum of Natural History. That means he is the head dinosaur paleontologist at the museum! Read on to find out more about Dr. Carrano and the dinosaurs he studies.

This *Ceratosaurus*, found in 1883, is Dr. Carrano's favorite fossil in the museum.

Dr. Carrano views his archives of bones.

What exactly do you do?

Like most paleontologists, there are three main things that I do. The first is field work. I discover new fossils and I bring them back to the museum. The second thing I do is study museum collections and research things that have already been discovered. The third thing I do is spend a lot of time in the library. It's very important to know what other researchers are doing and have done and to bring that knowledge to the study of your own fossils, so you can **MAKE NEW HYPOTHESES AND DRAW NEW CONCLUSIONS**.

When and why did you become interested in studying dinosaurs?

I became interested in dinosaurs when I was in second grade. My friend, Mike, was reading a book about dinosaurs from the school library, and I thought they were the most amazing things I had ever seen. I began to read all the dinosaur books I could find in the library. Then I started spending a lot of time in the Peabody Museum of Natural History in Connecticut, near where I lived. I think I found dinosaurs interesting because they were so incredible, but at the same time they were also real—**SCIENCE WITH ROOM FOR IMAGINATION**, too.

MATTHEW CARRANO

Every year Dr. Carrano spends time in the field looking for fossils.

What did it take to become a paleontologist?

It took a lot of studying and time in school. I went to college and learned about geology and biology, which are the two main subjects that paleontologists need most. I also learned how to conduct research and write scientific papers. Then I went to graduate school to learn more about paleontology, which took five and a half more years.

But what's most important for a paleontologist is to have **CURIOSITY, PATIENCE, A SHARP EYE,** and no fear of being wrong! All of science is built around taking ideas and trying to prove them wrong. Everyone has some ideas that, in the end, turn out to be incorrect. It's important not to feel too bad about being wrong, because by finding that out, you've made progress by eliminating one possible answer to your question.

What is your favorite fossil in the museum?

My favorite fossil in the museum is the skeleton of the predatory dinosaur *Ceratosaurus*. I like this fossil because it was the very first *Ceratosaurus* ever found—what scientists call the **TYPE SPECIMEN**—and was, in fact, the only specimen known for more than a hundred years. It's pretty complete for a dinosaur (maybe 75 percent of it is real). It also has some really unusual things about its skull, hands, and hips that make it interesting scientifically. For example, it has a short horn on its nose, which is very unusual for a predatory dinosaur.

Paleontologists use simple tools like these to carefully unearth their fossil finds.

Could there be dinosaur bones in my backyard?

There could be, but it depends on where you live. The important thing to remember is that **DINOSAURS LIVED EVERYWHERE ON EARTH** during the Mesozoic era—in every environment and on every continent. But when they died, only some environments were good for burying and preserving their bones so they could become fossils. And only some of those fossils are near enough to the surface for us to find. So when we look for dinosaur bones, we start in places where the geology tells us that the rocks are of the right age (between 65 and 230 million years old) and from the right kinds of environments (on land rather than underwater).

How often do you hunt for dinosaur bones, and how often do you find them when you are digging?

I usually spend a few weeks a year out in the field looking for dinosaur bones. I've traveled to South America and Africa to hunt for dinosaurs. Depending on where I go, I might find bones every day, or I might not find any at all. Sometimes I can go for days without finding anything, especially if I'm looking somewhere new where no one has found any fossils before. But in some places, fossils are scattered all over the ground.

I've been able to make many really exciting discoveries. When you're the person who gets to uncover a fossil for the first time, it's an amazing feeling to know that you're the first human being on Earth to lay eyes on that fossil. **THAT IS ALWAYS PRETTY INCREDIBLE.**

BELIEVE IT OR NOT!

Stegosaurus

Pteranodon

Ten Fascinating Dinosaur Facts to Make You Think

1 Dinosaurs were extremely successful creatures. They roamed the earth for more than 150 million years. Modern humans haven't even been around for a million years!

2 Dinosaurs lived all over the world in all kinds of environments, such as deserts, forests, and swamps. They even lived on Antarctica. At the time of the dinosaurs, the world was a much warmer place, and Antarctica was covered with lush forests.

3 Paleontologists think we've only uncovered about 10 percent of the dinosaur species that actually existed. That means there are probably thousands of dinosaur species yet to be discovered!

4 Dinosaurs died out 65 million years ago, but we see the relatives of dinosaurs everyday! Modern birds evolved from carnivorous dinosaurs related to *Tyrannosaurus rex.*

5 The long-necked dinosaur, *Apatosaurus*, died out 65 million years before *Tyrannosaurus rex* even came into existence. *T. rex* died out 62 million years before the earliest humans showed up!

6 Flying reptiles (like pterosaurs) and ocean reptiles (like plesiosaurs) lived at the same time as the dinosaurs, but they were not dinosaurs!

7 When dinosaurs roamed the earth, the continents were not where they are today. The continents were connected in one large landmass called Pangaea. Over millions of years, this landmass broke up and the continents slowly drifted apart. They are still on the move today. This process is known as plate tectonics.

8 One of the smallest known dinosaurs was the *Compsognathus*, which was about the size of a chicken. It was a carnivore that ate small vertebrates like lizards.

9 Mammals and dinosaurs lived at the same time, although early mammals tended to be very small, rodent-like animals. Only after dinosaurs died out did mammals start getting bigger.

10 Many dinosaur bones are found by people like you, not paleontologists. If you find a dinosaur bone, leave it where it is. Mark the exact location of the fossil on a map, and contact a museum. Maybe your fossil find will be a brand new dinosaur species!

CHECK OUT!
THE CASSOWARY IS A COUSIN OF THIS DINOSAUR. CAN YOU SEE THE FAMILY RESEMBLANCE? (SEE A CASSOWARY AT THE SMITHSONIAN'S NATIONAL ZOO!)

Tyrannosaurus

What?! I'm not a dinosaur?

Nope.

JOURNAL

Majungasaurus

Fossil Field Notes

My Favorite Fossil Find:

Where it was discovered:

Age:

Interesting information:

I really like this fossil because

I wonder

QUICK SKETCH

DRAW A SKETCH OF YOUR FAVORITE FOSSIL FIND:

DID YOU KNOW?

YOU CAN FIND FOSSILS ALL OVER THE MUSEUM.

THE *OCEAN HALL* HAS A BIG COLLECTION OF FOSSILIZED SEA LIFE, INCLUDING GIANT FOSSILIZED SHARK TEETH, ANCIENT WHALES, AND TRILOBITES OF ALL SHAPES AND SIZES.

THE *HALL OF HUMAN ORIGINS* HAS FOSSILIZED REMAINS OF OUR EARLY ANCESTORS, FROM *AUSTRALOPITHECUS* TO EARLY *HOMO SAPIENS*.

THE MINERAL AND GEMS GALLERY HAS A SLICE OF DINOSAUR BONE WITH AMETHYST CRYSTALS THAT FORMED INSIDE IT.

MAMMAL SAFARI

TIP!
USE THE LABELS WRITTEN IN FRONT OF THE DISPLAY CASES TO HELP YOU FIND THE MAMMALS YOU ARE LOOKING FOR.

MAMMALS COME IN ALL SIZES and they live in many different kinds of habitats, but there are three things they all have in common. All mammals have hair of some sort, they have tiny bones deep inside their ears that help them hear really well, and they are all nourished by their mother's milk when they are babies. You can learn a lot more about mammals in the **KENNETH E. BEHRING FAMILY HALL OF MAMMALS**.

Orientation Hall (the main entrance)

1 My name might trick people, but I don't really fly, I glide. Take a close look at the skin stretched between my front and hind legs and you'll see why. I can glide over 1,500 feet in a single soar. That's more than the length of five football fields!

2 You may think I'm a mammal imposter since I don't have any hair. The interesting thing is that I did have hair, but I lost it before I was born. Now I am sleek and smooth, which helps me to swim fast.

Africa

3 I am beautiful, sleek, and surprisingly strong. I drag my kill up a tree, even though it may weigh more than me. I have to take my dinner with me to protect it from the scavenging hyenas and lions.

4 Despite the fact that I weigh almost five tons, I am quite graceful—underwater. I can hold my breath for thirty minutes while I graze the river bed for food. I'm a relative of the pig, but I have large tusks in my huge mouth, so don't mess with me.

5 It can be a bit challenging to see in the thick vegetation of the African rainforest. That's why I have such bold white and black fur. It helps my troop see me in the trees, and it reminds my enemies that this is my territory.

I'll give you a head start!

Smile for the camera!

CHECK IT OUT!
GO EXPLORE *THE HALL OF MAMMALS* ONLINE!

Can you spot me in the museum?

A SCAVENGER HUNT IN THE HALL OF MAMMALS

Australia

6 I am a lesser-known member of the Australian marsupial club. My little *joey* is hanging out in my pouch right now. I might remind you of those famous Australians, the kangaroos, but I am special in my own way.

7 Even though I lay eggs and have a duck-like bill, I am a mammal. My bill is super sensitive. It helps me locate food underwater, even with my eyes closed tight.

South America

8 I am an expert at conserving my energy. I don't get a lot of nutrients from my diet of leaves. I hang from tree limbs with my hook-like claws, and I move very slowly. I even keep my body temperature cool to save energy.

9 I would be more than happy if you did not find me. I purposely try to blend into the dark jungle with my black coat. With my camouflage and my specialized eyes that help me see well in the dark, I am able to sneak up on my prey at night.

10 I don't look like many of my mammal cousins because of my armored covering, but, trust me, I am a mammal—I have a hairy belly. Have you seen my impressive claws? They help me dig around the forest floor for meals of insects and small animals.

I'm a glider not a flyer.

North America

11 You probably won't find me since I blend in so well with the arctic snow. I consider myself pretty lucky to have the warmest coat of all land mammals. I particularly like using my fluffy tail to keep my nose warm when I sleep. Back to my nap!

12 People often get my name wrong, but I hope you won't. My kind used to roam across the North American prairies in great herds, speckling the scenery brown with our furry coats. Despite my large, bulky size I can run fast—about 55 miles per hour. Unfortunately, we were hunted nearly to extinction. We still call the North American prairie home, and our numbers are slowly increasing.

I breathe air just like you!

Hey! I'm over here.

I lay eggs but I'm not a bird.

Answers: 1. Flying Squirrel 2. Risso's Dolphin 3. Leopard 4. Hippopotamus 5. Colobus Monkey 6. Red-necked Wallaby 7. Duck-billed Platypus 8. Three-toed Sloth 9. Jaguar 10. Giant Armadillo 11. Arctic Fox 12. Bison

If these mammals could talk, what would they tell you about themselves? **MATCH EACH MAMMAL TO ITS DESCRIPTION**.

AMAZI
MAMM
ADAPTAT

What's an *adaptation*, you ask? It's a special feature or behavior that helps an animal survive in its habitat.

Chimpanzee

Bat

Koala

Polar Bear

Opossum

Squirrel

Three-banded Armadillo

1. I have the ab... death when... play dead fo...

2. I am covered... of a bone-lik... into a perfec... from danger...

3. I make high-... move aroun... me "see" in... bounce off o...

4. Like all othe... front teeth t... That's a good... constantly w... gnawing on...

5. I am one of t... have learne... meal, I use lo... termites out... use stones t...

6. My sense of... strong. I can... hole from th... it is covered...

7. I have a spec... allows me to... eucalyptus le...

...nded Armadillo 3. Bat 4. Squirrel 5. Chimpanzee 6. Polar Bear 7. Koala

TRY THIS IN THE MUSEUM!

WRITE THE NAMES OF YOUR PICKS FOR THE AWARDS BELOW. ADD A QUICK DRAWING TOO, IF YOU WANT.

HALL OF MAMMALS AWARDS

With so many mammals, it's hard to pick favorites! But, here's your chance to decide which mammals deserve a special award.

BEST HAIRDO:

LARGEST MAMMAL:

MOST FIERCE MAMMAL:

MOST COLORFUL MAMMAL:

MOST BEAUTIFUL MAMMAL:

STRANGEST-LOOKING MAMMAL:

BEST ADAPTATION:

SMALLEST MAMMAL:

GRAND PRIZE BEST ALL-AROUND MAMMAL:

Camel

Bobcat

of Human Origins. Step back throu
and get up-close and personal w
your early ancestors.

THERE ARE MANY BIG QUESTIONS SCIENTISTS ARE TRYING TO ANSWER ABOUT HOW HUMANS DEVELOPED:

What exactly makes us human?

What is evolution and how does it happen?

Where did we come from?

What did our early ancestors and relatives look like? How did they compare to us?

Where are modern humans on the human family tree?

How are we related to other living things?

A
evo
wil
lik
m

Humans have hands that can make and use tools, from simple handaxes of long ago to complicated smartphones of today. What kinds of tools do you use in your everyday life?

Humans have large brains that can solve problems, store information, make quick decisions, think of new ideas, express emotions, and more. When was the last time your brain helped you out of a jam?

YOU PROBABLY HAVE SOME BIG QUESTIONS, TOO. HERE IS YOUR CHANCE TO LOOK AROUND AND DISCOVER SOME ANSWERS.

Humans can communicate by speaking and by using symbols, like the letters and words in this book! Speaking, reading, and writing are pretty complicated tasks. We can also express our thoughts through music and art. How do you like to express yourself?

HALL OF HUMAN ORIGINS MUST-SEE LIST:

- ☐ Travel back in time in the Time Tunnel —see how and where your ancient relatives lived.

- ☐ See a cast and a full-body reconstruction of a 3.2-million-year-old early human named Lucy.

- ☐ See the skeleton of a real Neanderthal who died from a wound that punctured his lung.

- ☐ Examine the life-size bronze sculptures of your early ancestors going about their daily lives.

- ☐ Get eye-to-eye with life-like reconstructions of more early ancestors and their relatives.

- ☐ Play a computer game to see what we might look like in another million years.

- ☐ Go on a field trip with scientists in three different interactive videos to see how early humans survived big challenges.

Humans rely on family and friends to be successful in life, especially when we are very small. Young and old alike, people need people. What are some things your family does for you that makes your life easier?

Humans are *bipedal*—that means we walk upright on two legs. This has enabled people to spread out all across the globe. It also means we can get around quickly in our everyday lives. Where have your legs taken you lately?

MILESTONES OF HUMAN EVOLUTION

Early humans begin walking upright.
What's so great about walking upright?
- It's easier to pick fruit from high branches.
- It frees up your hands to carry food, tools, and kids.
- You appear larger and more intimidating.
- You can move faster and more efficiently over greater distances.

6 MILLION YEARS AGO

New tools mean new foods.
How did tools change things for early humans?
- New tools led to new foods, like meat, which in turn meant better nutrition to fuel bigger brains and healthier bodies.
- Some of the earliest tools included handaxes, hammerstones, and fire. Fire was a big deal because cooking food—like meat— released nutrients, made it easier to eat, and killed parasites. Middle- and later- Stone Age tools included awls, burin, harpoons, arrowheads, spears, and needles.
- Tools came in handy for hunting, chopping, cutting, and scraping. They made work a lot easier!

Early humans used the sharp edges of hammerstones to remove meat from animal bones.

Lucy, a 3.2-million-year-old *Australopithecus afarensis*, walked upright on two feet but also climbed trees like her primate ancestors.

1.6 MILLION YEARS AGO

Brains get bigger quickly.
What caused the brain growth spurt?
- As humans spread around the globe, they faced more and more challenges in each new environment. The more problems early humans faced, the more they had to think to solve them. Solving problems sometimes meant the difference between life and death.
- Between about 800,000 and 200,000 years ago, the earth's climate was changing nearly constantly. This meant early humans constantly had to readjust—adjusting requires brains, so the brains of some early humans got bigger!

Brain endocasts, like these, show how much space is available inside a skull and help scientists measure brain size.

800,000 YEARS AGO

Humans begin farming.
Yes, this was a new idea 12,000 years ago!
- Farming led to groups of people settling down and starting communities where food and other resources were shared.
- Different communities traded with each other which led to cooperation and sometimes conflict.
- Farming was a turning point marking the beginning of modern human times.

12,000 YEARS AGO

Growing food changed everything for humans.

TRY THIS AT HOME!

See what kind of paleoanthropologist you would make **BY TAKING THIS POP QUIZ. YOUR JOB IS TO FIGURE OUT WHAT EACH OBJECT IS AND HOW IT WAS USED.**

WHAT IS IT? ARTIFACTS FROM EARLY HUMANS

Okay, it's time to think like a **PALEOANTHROPOLOGIST!**
PALEO means old, **ANTHRO** means man or human, and **OLOGIST** means someone who studies something. So a paleoanthropologist is someone who studies really old humans.

POP QUIZ

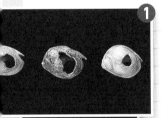

1
a. These are shells that may have been used as jewelry and for trade.
b. These are shells that may have been used for an early human baby rattle.
c. These are shells that may have been used to decorate ancient jack-o-lanterns.

2
a. It's an arrowhead, used for hunting.
b. It's a handaxe, used for cutting things like meat and wood.
c. It's the head of an ancient golf club.

3
a. It's a tool for removing tasty termites from termite mounds.
b. It's an early writing instrument.
c. It's an ancient flute for playing favorite old tunes.

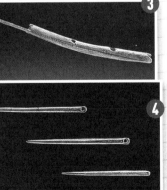

4
a. These are spears for hunting very small animals.
b. These are needles for sewing clothing used by ancient humans.
c. These are toothpicks for ancient humans.

5
a. It's an early human tool for weaving fabric.
b. It's a harpoon point for hunting fish.
c. It's a playing piece from an early human game.

PICK A FAVORITE!
WHAT WAS YOUR FAVORITE FIND IN THE *HALL OF HUMAN ORIGINS*? WHAT DO YOU THINK IT MEANS TO BE HUMAN? SHARE YOUR ANSWERS ON THE HUMAN ORIGINS WEBSITE!

Answers: 1. a 2. b 3. c 4. b 5. b

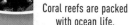
Coral reefs are packed with ocean life.

This strange looking deep-sea dweller is an anglerfish.

HERE ARE SOME INTERESTING OCEAN FACTS to get you started on your exploration of the deep.

THE OCEAN IS:

- essential to all life, including yours. Half of the oxygen we breathe comes from the ocean. Many other resources we need are found in the ocean as well—a lot of food, for example.

- one big body of water. Yes, technically we have the Atlantic, Pacific, Indian, and Arctic Oceans. But, if you think about it, they're all connected, making one big ocean!

- where life started. Scientists agree that the earliest life forms on Earth developed in the ocean billions of years ago. Life continued to evolve over billions of years, eventually branching out onto dry land.

- full of fascinating plants and animals. The ocean is home to whales, octopi, sharks, giant squid, glow-in-the-dark jellies, kelp forests, crabs, and coral, just to name a few.

- mostly unexplored. Most of our planet—71 percent of it—is covered by the ocean, and less than 5 percent of the ocean has been explored. There's a lot more to learn about this huge part of our planet!

- in need of your help. Our health and our planet's health depend on a healthy ocean. We need to protect the ocean from the effects of climate change, pollution, overfishing, and other human activities that put the ocean in danger.

OCEAN HALL MUST-SEE LIST

☐ Take a look at fossils from ancient ocean life, including the jaw of the giant shark, *Carcharodon megalodon.*

☐ Peek into a living coral reef. How many living creatures can you spot?

☐ Check out the giant Global Systems globe and learn how the ocean affects our climate and weather.

☐ Don't miss the preserved giant squid. This rarely seen animal was 36 feet long when it was alive!

☐ Watch a movie in the Ocean Explorer Theater that will take you to the darkest depths of the ocean.

☐ Meet Phoenix—the star of the hall—a life-size model of a 45-foot-long North Atlantic right whale. Read her story on page 66!

Jellies come in many beautiful colors, shapes, and sizes.

ZOOMING THROUGH THE OCEAN ZONES

CHECK IT OUT! WHILE IN THE OCEAN HALL, EXPLORE THE ZONES OF THE OCEAN JUST BEHIND PHOENIX. MEET THE CREATURES THAT HAVE ADAPTED TO LIVE IN EACH ZONE.

The Surface Zone Let the sun shine in!

This brightly lit zone stretches from the surface to about 660 feet (200 m) deep. That's just a little deeper than the Washington Monument is high.

This zone is full of tiny plant-like organisms called phytoplankton that turn sunlight into food. They also release HUGE amounts of oxygen that bubble up to the surface and goes into the air for us to breathe.

It's hard to hide in the surface zone. Animals that live there have to swim fast, leave the area, or blend in to avoid being eaten.

A starfish is not a fish—it's an echinoderm. That is why it's better called a sea star.

The Twilight Zone It's getting dark down here!

This zone extends from about 660 feet (200 m) to about 3,280 feet (1,000 m) below the surface. That's almost as deep as five Washington Monuments stacked on top of each other.

Not much sunlight reaches this zone—it's pretty dark down there.

Most of the animals that live in this zone have the ability to make their own light. This is called *bioluminescence*.

There's not much food in the twilight zone, so many animals come up to the surface zone every night to eat. They head back home before dawn.

Scientists believe that 90% of animals in the open ocean can bioluminesce, or make light, like this jelly.

The Deep Zone Who turned off the lights?

This zone plunges from about 3,280 feet (1,000 m) all the way to the ocean floor, over two miles down, an average of 13,120 feet (4,000 m) below the surface. That's almost 24 Washington Monuments stacked on top of each other! Some areas of the ocean are much deeper. The deepest known spot is the Marianna Trench, which is about 35,840 feet (11,000 m) deep—that's about 7 miles deep, or a total of about 65 Washington Monuments stacked up! No sunlight reaches the deep zone. It's pitch black. It's also really cold—just above freezing. With all that water pushing down overhead, there's also intense pressure in the deep zone. Scientists once thought no life could survive in the deep ocean, but now we know that many strangely adapted creatures call the deep ocean home.

This Longnose Cat Shark lives in the deep ocean.

The Washington Monument is 555 feet (169 m) high. That's almost as tall as the ocean surface zone is deep—660 feet (200m)!

660 feet / 200 meters

3,280 feet / 1,000 meters

13,120 feet / 4,000 meters

TRY THIS IN THE MUSEUM!

Take a careful look up at Phoenix, the North Atlantic right whale. **CAN YOU SPOT THE FEATURES LISTED ON THE NEXT PAGE?**

MEET PHOENIX:

Who am I? My name is Phoenix. I'm a North Atlantic right whale, and I am the star of the Ocean Hall! I actually live in the Atlantic Ocean, but you can see a full-size model of me right here in the *Ocean Hall* —just look up!

Phoenix, a North Atlantic right whale, is one of the largest mammals on Earth.

WHAT IS SO SPECIAL ABOUT ME? I'm a baleen whale, or a filter feeder. Do you see the long black pieces hanging from my upper jaw? That's my baleen. I use it to trap food. I take in huge gulps of water full of tiny sea creatures. The water filters through my baleen leaving behind tiny copepods (shrimp-like animals the size of a grain of rice) for me to eat. I spend about 18 hours a day feeding. I need about 2,200 pounds of food a day! You would too, if you weighed 140,000 pounds!

Unfortunately, my kind are highly endangered. **FEWER THAN 500 OF US REMAIN** in the North Atlantic Ocean today. A long time ago we were considered the "right" whales to hunt because we provided a lot of oil (from our melted blubber) and other valuable resources. We were hunted to the brink of extinction. Today it is illegal to hunt right whales, but we are still in danger. Sometimes we are hit by large ships, or we get tangled in commercial fishing gear. I was tangled up once, but, luckily, I got away.

DID YOU KNOW?

RIGHT WHALES HAVE NO KNOWN NATURAL PREDATORS. HUMAN ACTIVITIES ARE THEIR BIGGEST THREAT.

AT ONE TIME, RIGHT WHALE BLUBBER WAS BOILED DOWN TO MAKE OIL. FOR HUNDREDS OF YEARS, THE OIL WAS USED AS FUEL FOR LAMPS AND HEAT.

When whales are spotted ships are required to slow down and keep their distance.

Each North Atlantic right whale must be carefully tracked so we can better protect them.

A TALE OF A WHALE

It took four years to create this 45-foot-long replica of Phoenix. Every detail, down to her whiskers and scars, is perfectly placed.

I WAS BORN IN 1987 and was first spotted with my mother, Stumpy, off the coast of Georgia. I have already had four calves of my own, and I continue to be seen swimming in the Atlantic Ocean today.

Scientists are able to identify me by my **UNIQUE PATTERN OF CALLOSITIES**. Callosities are the chunky, rough white patches of skin on my body. Each right whale has a different pattern of callosities that is as unique as fingerprints. Scientists take pictures and make drawings of the callosities on each whale they see and are able to use those drawings and pictures to recognize us.

CALLOSITIES

Small crustaceans, known as whale lice, live on the callosities of North Atlantic right whales.

CAN YOU SPOT THESE FEATURES ON PHOENIX?
✓ CHECK THE ONES YOU FIND

☐ Whiskers on my chin—I'm a mammal, like you. All mammals have hair on their bodies—for me, it's just a few whiskers.

☐ White scars on my lips and tail— I got these from my run-in with the fishing gear.

☐ My belly button—I have one just like you! This is where the umbilical cord connected me to my mother before I was born.

☐ My little eyes—Even though they are small, I have good vision. My sense of hearing is even better!

☐ My callosities—You can see even more callosities by looking down at me from one of the balconies on the second floor.

YOUR OWN OCEAN MEMORY BY FILLING IN THE BLANKS IN THE STORY BELOW.

Try doing it without reading the whole story first. Share your special memory with your family or friends when you finish.

OCEAN MEMORIES

Do you hear the ocean when you hold a shell to your ear?

Sharks have been around for more than 400 million years!

Did you know that some species of sea stars have 40 arms?

Ahh, it's .... again, which means my
(season)

family is spending .... days at the beach
(number)

in .... It's time for fun in the sun!
(state)

I made sure to pack my ....
(noun)

and ....; they always come
(noun)

in handy at the beach.

Today, I woke up bright and early at .... o'clock
(number)

to go snorkeling with .... I put on
(family member)

my .... and headed to the water.
(piece of clothing)

The water felt .... as I swam over
(adjective)

the coral reef. Within minutes, I started spotting ocean

creatures in the water all around me. The first thing I

noticed was a .... hiding in a coral cave.
(ocean animal)

As I swam along I was a little surprised when I realized a

.... was swimming
(ocean animal)

alongside me!

Snorkeling is a great way to spy on ocean life.

That was enough snorkeling for one day,

so we headed back to the shore to relax.

The rest of my family was waiting for us on the

beach. They had built a sand .... It was
(noun)

pretty impressive. .... had collected a
(family member)

bunch of .... that had washed up on
(plural nouns)

shore. They were really ....
(adjective)

We spent .... hours ....
(number)   (verb ending with -ing)

on the beach and .... in the water.
(verb ending with -ing)

That evening we were worn out and ready for bed.

That night I dreamed of .... and
(ocean animal, plural)

rested up for another day of making ....
(adjective)

ocean memories.

The clown fish loves to hide among sea anemones' tentacles. No joke!

Dolphins have great eyesight and hearing, but a poor sense of smell.

Did you know a sea turtle can't pull its head inside its shell?

OCEAN FINDS

Ocean Hall Field Notes

Favorite Ocean Hall Find:

Where it's from:

Interesting information:

I really like this find because

Hanging out at the beach? Why not build a giant sand castle?

WHAT'S THE BIG DEAL

Geologist and Volcanologist, Liz Cottrell, explains it all.

Native copper

Crystal quartz

Liz Cottrell is at work conducting experiments about how the Earth's core formed.

Granite

What is geology all about?

LIZ COTTRELL: Geology is about understanding what we see around us. Why is the West Coast of the United States plagued by earthquakes and not the East Coast? Why are the Himalayas the world's tallest mountains? Why do we find abundant coal in Pennsylvania but not in Florida? Why are emeralds green? What causes Old Faithful to be, well, faithful?

Geology is about understanding where we came from and where we are going. How and when did Earth form? Why is Earth the only planet in our solar system with life-giving liquid water at the surface? What was the climate like in the past, and what will it be like in the future?

To help them answer these questions, geologists analyze all kinds of things, including rocks, minerals, gems, tree rings, fossils, fresh water, sea water, ice cores, meteorites, interplanetary dust particles, shells, volcanic ash, satellite data, earthquakes, and sediments.

What's the difference between a rock, a mineral, and a gem?

Minerals are naturally occurring compounds that have their atoms arranged in a repeating pattern. Rocks are made up of minerals. A rock can be made of only one kind of mineral or can be a collection of many minerals. A gem is any mineral that has been selected for its beauty and then cut or polished for display.

For example, the rock granite is made up of many minerals. Have a look at a granite countertop and you will notice a huge selection of minerals of different shapes, colors, and textures. One of those minerals is quartz, which looks a little like glass. A particularly large, clear piece of quartz mineral might be cut and polished and used in jewelry. **THIS QUARTZ IS THEN A GEM.**

So, you're a volcanologist. That sounds like it might be the coolest job at the Smithsonian. But what is a volcanologist?

YES, IT IS THE COOLEST JOB!
Volcanoes exist because the rocks that make up the deep Earth melt as they come to the surface and the pressure decreases. That melted rock, known as magma, comes to the surface as lava and ash in volcanic eruptions. Being a volcanologist is like being a detective. The rocks that come out of volcanoes contain clues that help me understand the story of what's going on deep inside the earth.

ABOUT GEOLOGY?

DID YOU KNOW?
GEOLOGISTS HELP US TO MANAGE OUR NATURAL RESOURCES. THE STUDY OF GEOLOGY HAS ENABLED US TO GET THE EARTH MATERIALS THAT BUILD THE WORLD AROUND US. MANY OF THE GOODS WE USE EVERYDAY ARE MADE FROM OIL, METAL, AND OTHER NATURAL MATERIALS FOUND IN THE CRUST OF THE EARTH. THESE NATURAL RESOURCES ARE LIMITED IN SUPPLY, SO WE NEED TO USE THEM CAREFULLY!

Aluminium is the most abundant metal, in the Earth's crust.

Silicon is the main component of computer chips.

Smartphones are made up of over 56 different metals.

GEOLOGY FINDS

Do you go on scientific adventures to study volcanoes?

Yes. One of my favorites was going on a research cruise in the Pacific Ocean. On this cruise, we lowered a huge metal bucket to the seafloor. That's where there are chains of volcanoes erupting all the time. We hauled up the bucket and brought up fresh volcanic rocks that we could take back to our labs to study. We worked around the clock. But when you are doing science in a really intense way like this, **IT IS MAGICAL AND FUN.**

EXPLORE THE "DYNAMIC EARTH."
BUILD A VOLCANO, TOUR MINES, EXPLORE THE INNER EARTH, TAKE A PLANETARY TOUR, AND MORE!

Nighttime eruption of the Stromboli volcano in Italy

Visiting the Janet Annenberg Hooker Hall of Geology, Gems, and Minerals? DON'T MISS:

☐ The world-famous Hope Diamond. Why is it blue?

☐ The world's largest, flawless crystal ball. What will you see in the crystal ball?

☐ Earrings, necklaces, and crowns of kings and queens. Whose jewels will you find?

☐ A slice of a crystallized dinosaur bone. How did that happen?

☐ Minerals that look like mold, wood, and cotton candy. Which is your favorite?

☐ Glow-in-the-dark rocks. Why do they glow?

☐ Chunks of copper, silver, and gold. What makes these metals so valuable?

☐ A volcanic basalt "bomb." How did it form?

☐ A real seismograph for measuring the intensity of earthquakes. Will you witness an earthquake?

☐ Rocks from space. What's inside a meteorite?

THE TRUE STORY OF

TRY THIS AT HOME! READ ALL ABOUT THE HOPE DIAMOND, THEN SKETCH IT AND TRY THE POP QUIZ ON THE OPPOSITE PAGE.

The Hope Diamond today. Have you seen it?

Washington socialite Evalyn Walsh McLean wears the Hope Diamond.

THE HOPE DIAMOND has had a mighty long journey from its original home deep in the earth to its current home in the Smithsonian National Museum of Natural History. Formed over a billion years ago, it was uncovered in a mine in India almost 400 years ago. From the moment it was found, people knew it was something special. Like all diamonds, the Hope Diamond was rough and uncut, not shiny or sparkly, when it was found. But it was huge—nearly the size of a golf ball! And it was not clear, or "white," like common diamonds—it was blue. After it was cut and polished, it's rare dark blue color was even more breathtaking.

Since its discovery, the blue diamond has been sold a great many times and even stolen once! It belonged to kings and queens, as well as to plain old rich folks around the world. It was cut and re-cut taking it from its **ORIGINAL SIZE OF OVER 112 CARATS** (the size of a golf ball) to its present size of 45.52 carats.

Some say there is a **CURSE OF BAD LUCK** connected to the Hope Diamond. Throughout history there have been many tragic stories told about its owners being murdered, jailed, injured, and more.

FEAR NOT. Most historians who have studied the story of the Hope Diamond are pretty sure that the curse and tales of woe were made up by a clever jewelry salesman trying to appeal to a special buyer who liked "unlucky" objects.

That special buyer was a ritzy Washington, DC, socialite named Evalyn Walsh McLean. Evalyn was a wealthy woman with a weakness for fine jewels and a belief that objects that were unlucky for others were lucky for her. She owned the Hope Diamond from 1911 until she died in 1947. She wore it like a special badge of honor, and some say she even let her dog wear it on his collar from time-to-time.

CHECK IT OUT! THE HOPE DIAMOND GLOWS AFTER EXPOSURE TO UV LIGHT. THIS IS CALLED *PHOSPHORESCENCE* (FOSS-FOR-RESS-ENSE). SEE IT HERE!

Wow!

THE HOPE DIAMOND

A man named Harry Winston bought Evalyn's entire jewelry collection after her death, including the Hope Diamond. Eventually, he donated it to the Smithsonian Institution to start a national gem collection. In 1958, Mr. Winston mailed the Hope Diamond to the Smithsonian in a brown paper package!

Today **THE HOPE DIAMOND BELONGS TO YOU!** Yes, as a part of the Smithsonian's gem collection, the diamond belongs to the people of the United States. But don't get your hopes up. You won't be wearing the Hope Diamond anytime soon. And neither will your dog!

This is the brown paper package that the Hope Diamond arrived in.

POP QUIZ

SKETCH THE HOPE DIAMOND HERE:

QUICK SKETCH

DID YOU KNOW?
THE HOPE DIAMOND WAS ONCE CALLED THE "FRENCH BLUE." IT GOT ITS CURRENT NAME FROM A PREVIOUS OWNER, A WEALTHY ENGLISH BANKER NAMED HENRY PHILIP HOPE. IF YOU COULD GIVE IT A NEW NAME, WHAT WOULD YOU CALL IT?

1. How much does the Hope Diamond weigh?
   a. about 25 carats
   b. about 45 carats
   c. about 105 carats

2. What is a carat?
   a. the price of a precious gemstone
   b. a unit for measuring the weight of a precious stone
   c. a crunchy orange vegetable

3. What gives the Hope Diamond its blue color?
   a. a very small amount of boron inside the diamond
   b. a special blue light that shines on the diamond
   c. blue food coloring

Answers: 1. b 2. b 3. a

FIND SOME PRICELESS TREASURES USING THE CLUES BELOW. Write the name of each of your finds on the line after its matching clue. Get your family or friends to help you! START IN *THE MINERALS AND GEMS GALLERY*.

TREASURE HUNTING

2

My metallic shine has fooled many people over the years. I'm not composed of the element gold, like folks tend to think. I'm actually a combination of iron and sulfur, and I can grow in a variety of shapes and sizes. Do you know what I'm called?

....

1

The ancient Greeks didn't know what I was. They thought I was water frozen so solid that I couldn't melt. But I am not made of water. I am made up of a special combination of silicon and oxygen. What am I?

....

I was studied intensely by James Smithson, the man for whom the Smithsonian is named. I was named after him, too. I was first discovered in New Mexico and am a pleasing turquoise color. What's my name?

....

3

4

I am a mineral that comes in many colors. I am very hard. Only diamonds are harder. I can be cut into precious gemstones, including rubies, if I am red, and sapphires, if I am blue. What am I?

....

IN THE GEMS AND MINERALS GALLERY

6

Based on my shaggy appearance, you might not believe that I am a mineral. I was once used as a building material because I am strong and fire resistant. People now know that I can cause health problems if you inhale my fibrous crystals into your lungs. Find my name.

I look a bit like fuzzy white mold, don't you think? I'm actually a mineral that was found in Bombay, India. I formed in the cavity of a rock. Can you find me?

5

7

8

My crystals are so soft they can be scratched with a fingernail. I can grow in long, straight formations; thin, flat plates; and sharp needles. But people are most impressed when I form like a twisted rope. This happens when parts of me grow faster than other parts. What mineral am I?

My unique arrangement of atoms causes many colors to flash off my surface like fire. I am found in many places on Earth, but some of the most beautiful samples can be found in Australia. If your birthday is in October, I am your birthstone. What am I called?

Answers: 1. Quartz 2. Pyrite 3. Smithsonite 4. Corundum 5. Okenite 6. Asbestos 7. Opal 8. Gypsum

TRY THIS AT HOME!

FOLLOW THE INSTRUCTIONS BELOW TO START YOUR OWN ROCK COLLECTION.

START YOUR OV

Step 1: Collect Some Rocks

1. Ask an adult to go rock hunting with you. Try to collect rocks found in natural settings, such as along a river bank, or on the forest floor, rather than rocks that have been moved by humans, like rocks in driveways.

TIP!
YOU SHOULD PROBABLY ONLY COLLECT ROCKS YOU ARE ABLE TO CARRY.

2. Place your finds in individual plastic zipper bags. But first, use a permanent marker to label each bag with the date and where you found the rock.

Step 2: Organize and Study Your Rocks

1. Clean your rocks in a bucket of soapy water. Do they look different all cleaned up?

2. After the rocks are totally dry, paint a small patch on each rock with white correction fluid. After it dries, write a number on the white patch with your permanent marker.

3. In your notebook, record the number for each rock, as well as the date and location where you found it. Add other important information such as the size, color, texture, and shape of each rock. Check out the sample notebook entry on the right.

4. Use your rock identification guide to see if you can identify your rocks or the minerals in your rocks. Get an adult to help you with this if you have trouble. To learn more about your rocks do some online research by searching for the phrases "rock identification key" and "mineral identification key."

TIP!
ROCKS THAT TURN TO MUD WHEN YOU WASH THEM ARE CALLED MUD.

5. Store your rocks in individual small boxes, egg cartons, plastic trays, or on a special shelf.

Step 3: Sort and Di Your Collec

1. You can sort your rocks any way you'd like, including by color, size, texture, shape, type, or anything else you can think of.

STORING
IS GOOD.
TO G

2. Choose some rocks to display in a place (you don't need to display e your collection). You can even crea describing the rocks.

3. Arrange your display and invite yo family to check out your exhibit. B answer questions about your rock your visitors will be curious!

TIP!
DO NOT PUT ROCKS IN YOUR PARENTS' WASHING MACHINE.

Rock Collection Log

Rock#:	Date Found:
Color:	Texture:
Description/Other Notes:	

ROCK COLLECTION

You will need...

Why collect rocks?

- Rocks hold secrets about how the earth was formed, where glaciers flowed, how environments changed, and what creatures roamed where. Once you start learning about rocks, you can begin to understand their stories.

- You can find rocks just about anywhere. They are in your backyard, in the woods, and in the park. You don't have to travel to an exotic land to find rocks (but you can!).

- Rocks are free, unless you decide to buy some special samples.

- Making a collection is fun, and it's cool to display your collection for your friends and family to see.

- You can become a geologist-in-training by collecting and studying rocks.

A NOTEBOOK FOR RECORDING INFORMATION ABOUT YOUR FINDS

EGG CARTONS OR SMALL BOXES FOR STORING AND DISPLAYING YOUR ROCKS

A ROCK FIELD GUIDE FOR IDENTIFYING YOUR ROCKS, LIKE *SMITHSONIAN HANDBOOKS: ROCKS & MINERALS BY CHRIS PELLANT*

White Correction Fluid

A PERMANENT MARKER AND WHITE CORRECTION FLUID FOR LABELING YOUR ROCKS (ASK AN ADULT TO HELP YOU FIND THESE)

A SMALL SHOVEL FOR DIGGING UP ROCKS

BONUS IDEA!
Turn some of your rocks into PET ROCKS!

A BUNCH OF SMALL PLASTIC ZIPPER BAGS

A MAGNIFYING GLASS FOR LOOKING AT THE DETAILS OF YOUR ROCKS

A BACKPACK FOR HOLDING YOUR ROCKS WHEN YOU ARE OUT COLLECTING

A BUCKET, DISH SOAP, AND WATER FOR CLEANING YOUR ROCKS

RULE!

Longwing Butterfly

There are more species of arthropods—also known as bugs—than all the other kinds of animal life on Earth combined! Nine out of every 10 animals that roam the earth are arthropods.

But what exactly is an **ARTHROPOD**? **ARTHRO** means jointed and **POD** means foot. All arthropods have jointed legs. They also have something else in common—an **EXOSKELETON**. That's a skeleton on the outside of their body. To grow, arthropods have to shed—or molt—their exoskeletons and grow new, bigger ones. What do you think you would look like with your skeleton outside your body?

The arthropod group includes **INSECTS**, **ARACHNIDS** (such as spiders and scorpions), centipedes and millipedes, and **CRUSTACEANS** (such as crabs and lobsters). Arthropods come in all sizes, from crabs with 12-foot arm spans to so small that you can't see them without a microscope.

Arthropods can be found **EVERYWHERE** on Earth, from the highest mountain peaks to the deepest parts of the ocean. But how can arthropods live in so many different environments? Because arthropods **EVOLVED** adaptions (features/traits) over 500 million years to a variety of very different conditions, there is a huge variety of species.

Arthropods live **UNDERWATER**, in the **WOODS**, in the **DESERT**, in **HIVES**, in **MOUNDS**, on **WEBS**, and on other animals. They even live in **BUILDINGS**, like the National Museum of Natural History! Why not see what arthropods you can find in the **O. ORKIN INSECT ZOO**.

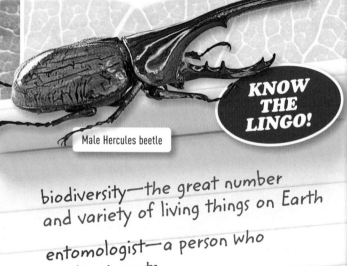

Male Hercules beetle

KNOW THE LINGO!

biodiversity—the great number and variety of living things on Earth

entomologist—a person who studies insects

entomophagy—the practice of eating insects (yes, many human cultures around the world enjoy entomophagy)

INSECT ZOO MUST-SEE LIST

- [ ] A tarantula feeding—ask a volunteer what time!
- [ ] A life-size African termite mound that you can crawl through
- [ ] A working beehive with a tunnel to the outdoors
- [ ] Watch butterflies and moths emerge from their chrysalides and cocoons in the emergence chamber.
- [ ] Ants that store honey!
- [ ] Four different habitats and the bugs that call them home—a mangrove swamp, a rainforest, a desert, and a pond
- [ ] And, of course, over 60 species of live arthropods for you to observe up-close!

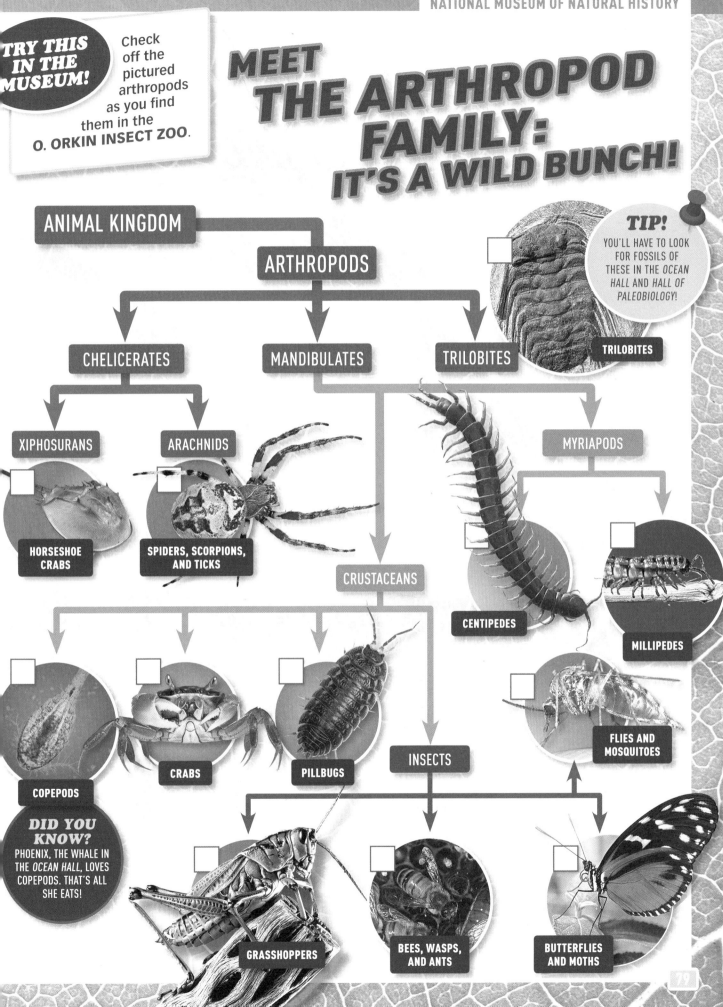

MEET THE ARTHROPOD FAMILY: IT'S A WILD BUNCH!

TIP! YOU'LL HAVE TO LOOK FOR FOSSILS OF THESE IN THE *OCEAN HALL* AND *HALL OF PALEOBIOLOGY*!

ANIMAL KINGDOM

ARTHROPODS

CHELICERATES

MANDIBULATES

TRILOBITES

TRILOBITES

XIPHOSURANS

ARACHNIDS

MYRIAPODS

HORSESHOE CRABS

SPIDERS, SCORPIONS, AND TICKS

CENTIPEDES

MILLIPEDES

CRUSTACEANS

COPEPODS

CRABS

PILLBUGS

INSECTS

FLIES AND MOSQUITOES

DID YOU KNOW? PHOENIX, THE WHALE IN THE *OCEAN HALL*, LOVES COPEPODS. THAT'S ALL SHE EATS!

GRASSHOPPERS

BEES, WASPS, AND ANTS

BUTTERFLIES AND MOTHS

FAVORITE ARTHROPOD FINDS

TRY THIS IN THE MUSEUM!

With over 60 species of live arthropods to discover in the *O. Orkin Insect Zoo,* you should be able to find some of these cool bugs. **WRITE THEIR NAMES IN THE BOXES BELOW AND DRAW A QUICK FIELD SKETCH** of your favorites.

...ican ...ant ...ipede

Desert Hairy Scorpion

Madagascar Hissing Cockroach

HAS FUZZY LEGS:

LOOKS LIKE A LEAF:

CAN SWIM UNDERWATER:

SPINS A WEB:

LIVES IN MY HOME:

HAS ITS OWN EXIT FROM THE INSECT ZOO TO THE OUTDOORS:

HAS STRONG PINCHERS AND A TAIL THAT CAN STING:

LIVES IN AN UNDERGROUND BURROW:

BACKYARD BIODIVERSITY

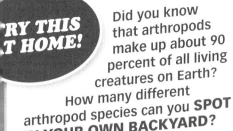

TRY THIS AT HOME! Did you know that arthropods make up about 90 percent of all living creatures on Earth? How many different arthropod species can you SPOT **IN YOUR OWN BACKYARD?**

Here's what to do:

Step 1: Head outside to your backyard or a nearby park, and start looking for bugs! You can spot them just about anywhere.

Step 2: When you find one, be sure to observe with your eyes only. Don't disturb an arthropod in its habitat. Use a magnifying glass to get a close-up look.

Step 3: Make a quick field sketch in your notebook, or take a photograph of the bug so you can try to identify it later.

Step 4: Write down the following observations:

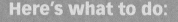

1. Describe its body:

2. Describe where it lives:

3. Describe what it is doing:

4. Describe any other interesting observations you make:

Here's what ⟶ **you need**

NOTEBOOK AND PENCIL

CAMERA (OPTIONAL)

MAGNIFYING GLASS

Insect identification guidebook

INSECT IDENTIFICATION GUIDEBOOK

TIP!
YOU CAN USE AN IDENTIFICATION GUIDE OR THE ARTHROPOD FAMILY TREE ON PAGE 79 TO GET A BETTER IDEA OF WHAT KINDS OF BUGS CALL YOUR BACKYARD HOME!

OR TRY THIS ONLINE IDENTIFICATION GUIDE

Butterfly

THE DISCOVERY ROOM AND Q?RIUS

Man-made artifacts help tell the story of human civilizations.

DO YOU WANT TO GET YOUR HANDS ON SOME OBJECTS FROM THE MUSEUM'S COLLECTIONS?

ARE YOU READY TO PRACTICE YOUR SKILLS AS A SCIENTIST?

ARE YOU ITCHING TO TRY OUT SOME HIGH-TECH SCIENTIFIC TOOLS?

DO YOU WANT TO SEE SOME SCIENTISTS AT WORK AND GET A CHANCE TO CHAT WITH THEM ABOUT IT?

High-powered microscopes make scientific observation fun!

The museum has miles of specimen-packed shelves like these to store its massive collection.

So wait... there's even MORE stuff to explore?

On the **FIRST FLOOR**, behind the *Ocean Hall*, is **THE DISCOVERY ROOM** where you can:

- touch museum artifacts and specimens;
- use tools like microscopes, magnifiers, and x-ray light boxes;
- take a break and read a book about your favorite natural history finds; and
- explore collection drawers—find out what is hidden inside!

On the **GROUND FLOOR**, you will find **Q?RIUS**, where you can:

- get into the collections! Over 20,000 objects are available for you to touch and observe;
- use real tools that real scientists use, like compound microscopes;
- watch scientists at work in the lab and in the field and talk to them about the interesting things they do;
- make your own field books to share with your friends and family; and
- learn what goes on behind the scenes at the museum.

YOUR TICKET TO SCIENTIFIC EXPLORATION!

JOURNAL

What was your favorite find in the Discovery Room?

Write about it, or draw a quick field sketch here.

Bones, like this human skull, always have stories to tell.

Scientists from around the world can use the museum's collection to help answer their questions.

What did you uncover in Q?RIUS?

Write about it, or draw a quick field sketch here.

There is so much to see at the museum!

TRY THIS AT HOME!

Design your own postcard for the Smithsonian **NATIONAL MUSEUM OF NATURAL HISTORY**. Then write a few lines to yourself about your visit here! **WHAT DO YOU WANT TO REMEMBER?**

WHAT DI

What did you think of National Mus of Natural Hist Quite a collect huh?

The National Museum of Natural History

Did you see the Tyrannosaurus rex foss the Hall of Paleobiolog

CHECK IT OUT!
BE SURE TO CHECK OUT THE AWESOME ADVENTURES AT THE SMITHSONIAN: THE OFFICIAL KIDS GUIDE TO THE SMITHSONIAN WEBSITE. IT'S PACKED WITH ALL KINDS OF AT-HOME ACTIVITIES, RESOURCES, AND FUN BONUS MATERIAL FOR YOU TO EXPLORE!

Dear Me,

Me!

My street!

My town!

My country!

Love, Me

YOU THINK?

THINK FAST!

Did you see any bats hanging around in the *Hall of Mammals*?

20 QUESTIONS: After your visit to the National Museum of Natural History, answer these questions as fast as you can!

1. Was this your first time visiting the Smithsonian National Museum of Natural History?   YES/NO

2. How many hours were you at the museum?

3. Did you check out the African elephant and all of the other creatures around its feet?   YES/NO

4. Did you find Phoenix's belly button?   YES/NO

5. Did you see any glowing ocean life?   YES/NO

6. Did you watch the fish swimming in the live coral reef?   YES/NO

7. Did you gaze into the eyes of your early ancestors?   YES/NO

8. Did you find any giant dinosaur fossils?   YES/NO

9. Did you imagine a *T. rex* alive?   YES/NO

10. Did you find any mammals you wanted to take home with you?   YES/NO

11. Did you find any mammals that you wouldn't want to run into in the wild?   YES/NO

12. Did you fight the crowds to see the Hope Diamond?   YES/NO

13. Were you impressed by the hundreds—or was it thousands—of minerals?   YES/NO

14. Did you touch any insects?   YES/NO

15. Did you meet any butterflies?   YES/NO

16. Did you catch an IMAX movie?   YES/NO

17. Did you check out the Discovery Room?   YES/NO

18. Did you visit Q?RIUS?   YES/NO

19. Do you think you might be a scientist someday?   YES/NO

20. What would you study?

There's always something new here at the museum!

WHAT'S NEW?
IF YOU ARE WONDERING WHAT'S COMING NEXT TO THE NATIONAL MUSEUM OF NATURAL HISTORY, BE SURE TO VISIT THE MUSEUM WEBSITE OFTEN.

Did any butterflies land on you in the Butterfly Pavilion?

THINGS TO SEE AND DO AT THE NATIONAL MUSEUM OF AMERICAN HISTORY:

☐ See the first car to drive all the way across the United States—a cherry-red Winton in *America on the Move*.

☐ Gaze at the original Star-Spangled Banner, preserved in a special environmentally-controlled chamber located on the second floor.

☐ Find the portable desk used by Thomas Jefferson when he wrote the Declaration of Independence in *The American Presidency: A Glorious Burden*.

☐ See a selection of dresses worn by First Ladies and learn about their important contributions in *The First Ladies*.

☐ Visit a full-sized house moved to the museum from Massachusetts and uncover the stories of its former inhabitants in *Within These Walls*....

☐ Get lost in *The Miniature World of Faith Bradford*, a five-story doll house with 23 rooms and more than 1,000 mini-treasures.

☐ See wartime objects in *The Price of Freedom: Americans at War* including George Washington's sword and scabbard, a World War II Willys Jeep, and a Huey helicopter used in Vietnam.

☐ Discover treasures from the United States' earliest days to today, from a fragment of the Plymouth Rock to Dorothy's ruby slippers, in *American Stories*.

☐ Find interactive carts stationed throughout the museum and touch the objects the museum educators have to share with you. (Check at the Welcome Center for times and locations.)

☐ Practice non-violent protest techniques at the Greensboro lunch counter. (Check at the Welcome Center for times of Historic Theater programs.)

WELCOME TO THE NATIONAL MUSEUM OF AMERICAN HISTORY

If objects could talk, just imagine the stories they could tell! What do you think George Washington's uniform would tell you about our first president? Or what would Dorothy's ruby slippers tell us about the making of the movie *The Wizard of Oz*? What would your belongings tell others about you? Here at the **NATIONAL MUSEUM OF AMERICAN HISTORY**, objects do tell stories. They don't actually speak, of course, but the many curators who work behind-the-scenes at the museum act as interpreters to tell their stories for them. Get ready to discover tales from America's past— tales of courage, hard work, exploration, and adventure—that together tell the larger story of the United States of America since it was formed over two hundred years ago.

People have stories to tell, too—stories about our lives and the people, places, and things in our lives. When we tell our stories, we leave history in our path. Yes, even you are making history. Each day that goes by is another day that adds to the sum of your life story— your history.

When we hear stories from the past, we can start to understand what life was like for a group of people, a town, a city, a state, or a country during a certain period of time. These stories become our history, **THE STORY OF US**.

This museum has thousands of fun, interesting—even amazing—objects in its collection. You'll find everything from First Lady Michelle Obama's ball gown and President Abraham Lincoln's top hat to a bunch of kids' lunch boxes, a big green locomotive, and the Star-Spangled Banner, the flag that inspired the national anthem. These are all things that people have used over the years, but history is more than just the objects themselves. It's the stories about these things and the people connected to them, and it's what the objects mean to us today.

GO EXPLORE THIS FASCINATING PLACE. Let your curiosity lead the way. Look closely, and read about the things you find. What do they tell you? Follow the paths of history that take you all over this museum, and see where you end up.

What's the story?

JOURNAL

What are you most excited to see at the National Museum of American History?

AMERICAN HISTORY

The National Museum of American History is renovating the West Wing of the building to provide its visitors even more fantastic exhibitions! It's a big job and is going to take some time. You can check the website before your visit or stop by the Welcome Center when you arrive for the most up-to-date map information.

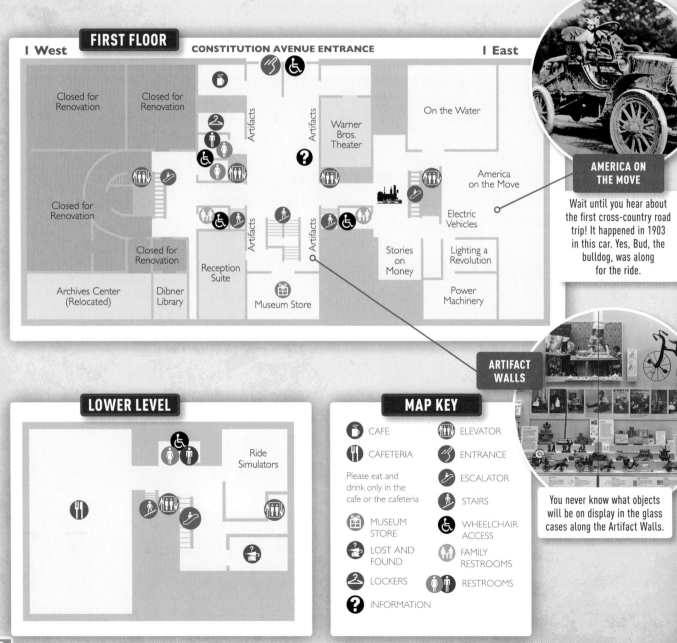

FIRST FLOOR

| West   CONSTITUTION AVENUE ENTRANCE   East

- Closed for Renovation
- Closed for Renovation
- Artifacts
- Artifacts
- Warner Bros. Theater
- On the Water
- Closed for Renovation
- Closed for Renovation
- Reception Suite
- Artifacts
- Artifacts
- America on the Move
- Electric Vehicles
- Stories on Money
- Lighting a Revolution
- Archives Center (Relocated)
- Dibner Library
- Museum Store
- Power Machinery

AMERICA ON THE MOVE

Wait until you hear about the first cross-country road trip! It happened in 1903 in this car. Yes, Bud, the bulldog, was along for the ride.

ARTIFACT WALLS

You never know what objects will be on display in the glass cases along the Artifact Walls.

LOWER LEVEL

- Ride Simulators

MAP KEY

- CAFE
- CAFETERIA

Please eat and drink only in the cafe or the cafeteria

- MUSEUM STORE
- LOST AND FOUND
- LOCKERS
- INFORMATION
- ELEVATOR
- ENTRANCE
- ESCALATOR
- STAIRS
- WHEELCHAIR ACCESS
- FAMILY RESTROOMS
- RESTROOMS

Did you know there is an entire two-story house inside the museum? It sounds crazy, but it's true! Visit the house from 16 Elm Street.

WITHIN THESE WALLS...

The Star-Spangled Banner is America's flag, national anthem, and a legendary story all rolled into one.

THE STAR-SPANGLED BANNER

SECOND FLOOR

2 West | **2 East**

- Closed for Renovation
- Within These Walls...
- Star-Spangled Banner
- American Stories
- Flag Hall
- Documents Gallery
- Artifacts
- Museum Store
- Closed for Renovation
- Welcome Center
- African American History and Culture Gallery

GREENSBORO LUNCH COUNTER

Do you have a question? Do you want to find out what's new? Stop by and chat with the friendly folks in the Welcome Center.

WELCOME CENTER

THE NATIONAL MALL ENTRANCE

Yes, even presidents wear pajamas. You can see these silk PJ's worn by President Warren G. Harding in the exhibit American Presidency: A Glorious Burden.

THE AMERICAN PRESIDENCY

THIRD FLOOR

3 West | **3 East**

- Closed for Renovation
- Closed for Renovation
- Closed for Renovation
- Open to Flag Hall
- First Ladies
- American Presidency
- Museum Store
- Gunboat *Philadelphia*
- Price of Freedom

Learn more about America at war in the *Price of Freedom* exhibit.

PRICE OF FREEDOM

I WANT YOU for the U.S. ARM ENLIST NOW

FIRST LADIES

Examine the gowns and accessories worn by the First Ladies and get a glimpse of their lives in the White House.

Uncle Sam wants you! Over 16 million US troops served in World War II. Many of them enlisted voluntarily, but most were drafted by "Uncle Sam."

A PEAK INTO

The *Artifact Walls* at the National Museum of American History, which can be seen on the first floor, are an ever-changing display of treasures pulled from the museum's miles of storage shelves. Each object on display has a story to tell.

Toys from ....
1825–1939

Artifact name: ....

I chose this because ....

....

Artifact name: ....

I chose this because ....

....

Artifact name: ....

I chose this because ....

....

Artifact name: ....

I chose this because ....

....

AMERICA'S TREASURES

JOURNAL

What artifacts did you like best? Why?

Find something you have never seen before.
What can you figure out about it?

Name something of yours that you would like to see displayed
on the *Artifact Walls*? What story would it tell about you?

Hmm...

LANDM

TRY THIS IN THE MUSEUM!

SEE HOW MANY LANDMARKS YOU CAN SPOT IN THE MUSEUM.

A landmark is a pl
special meaning, li
really old tree in a
National Museum of
seen landmarks w
Why do you thi
LANDMARKS?

What happened
at the Greensboro

OF AMERICAN HISTORY

How did this draft wheel work?

Would you volunteer to fight in a war? During the Civil War, many people did volunteer, but there were not enough soldiers to fill the ranks. That's where this object came in. It's a *draft wheel*. The names of men were written on slips of paper and put inside the hollow middle. Around and around it spun, and around and around went the fates of the men whose names spun inside. Each man whose name was pulled out went off to fight in America's deadliest conflict, unless he was rich enough to pay someone to take his place.

The Civil War draft wheel is on 3, East.

What was so special about the John Bull locomotive?

In 1831, the year this locomotive was shipped to the United States, major changes were in store for the country. The railroad was about to permanently alter the landscape of America, connecting cities like never before. This was one of the first steam locomotives to arrive on the scene. A young steamboat mechanic named Isaac Dripps had the honor of putting it together when it arrived from England. It was a very hard job because before it was shipped it was taken apart into many pieces. Isaac got no instructions on how to put it back together. But he was a smart fellow and was up for the challenge. He had it ready to run the rails in a few weeks. And run the rails it did. This train spent many years carrying passengers and cargo between the big cities of Philadelphia and New York City on the Camden and Amboy Railroad.

The John Bull locomotive is on 1, East.

TEST YOUR DETECTIVE SKILLS BY TAKING THIS POP QUIZ!

WHAT IN THE WORLD IS THAT?

There is a good chance that you will **NOT** see these items on display in the National Museum of American History. Only a fraction of the museum's collection is on view at any given time. When not on view, objects are stored **BEHIND THE SCENES**.

WHAT ARE THESE MYSTERIOUS FINDS?

POP QUIZ

1 LEECHES

2 Ball PERFECT MASON

3

4

1. It must be:
   a. a jar of leeches, once considered a tasty dessert in regions of the United States.
   b. a jar holding the ashes of someone's pet dog named Leeches.
   c. a jar of leeches, once used to suck blood from the bodies of sick people.

2. I think this is:
   a. a mousetrap with a funnel on top that let mice in, and prongs that kept them from escaping.
   b. a contraption used to separate egg whites from egg yolks.
   c. a gadget used to grow salt crystals for school science fair projects.

3. This could be:
   a. a tool for scraping dirt from the bottom of a horse's hooves.
   b. two lead minie ball bullets that crashed into each other during battle.
   c. a once-fancy piece of jewelry that melted in a fire at the White House in 1814.

4. This looks like:
   a. a dresser of drawers for an extremely large family.
   b. a storage cabinet for kitchen supplies, including utensils and spices.
   c. a cabinet for holding cards that helped people find books in libraries.

MUSEUM OF ME!

TRY THIS AT HOME!

DRAW ITEMS YOU WOULD FEATURE IN YOUR VERY OWN "MUSEUM OF ME."

MY MUSEUM OF ME!

What do your belongings say about you? If you were to create a museum all about you, what would you display? You are a unique person with hobbies, habits, likes, and dislikes. Which of your belongings would tell your story? **IT'S YOUR MUSEUM—YOU DECIDE!**

TO SHOW
WHERE I LIVE:

TO SHOW
WHAT I LIKE TO
DO FOR FUN:

TO SHOW
WHAT SPORTS OR
HOBBIES I LIKE:

TO SHOW
HOW I LIKE
TO DRESS:

TO SHOW MY
FAVORITE SUBJECT
IN SCHOOL:

TO SHOW
SPECIAL TRADITIONS
IN MY LIFE:

TO REPRESENT
MY FAMILY:

PORTRAIT
OF ME:

Pop Quiz Answers: **1. C: Jar of bloodsucking leeches**—For centuries, doctors used leeches to suck blood from sick patients and purchased them from pharmacists who kept them in jars like this one. Aren't you glad doctors do not use them today for medical procedures? **2. A: Mousetrap**—This mousetrap is one example of more than 4,400 that have received patents for the U.S. Patent Office. Could you design a better one? **3. B: Two lead minie ball bullets**—During the Civil War in December 1862 at the Battle of Fredericksburg, these two minie balls flew from opposite sides of the battlefield and collided in midair. What are the chances of this occurrence happening again? **4. C: Library card catalog**—Not long ago, every library had cabinets like this one to hold thousands of catalog cards – arranged in alphabetical order by title, author and subject – for locating books.

TRY THIS AT HOME!

Do you know the "Star-Spangled Banner?" Can you sing the first verse? **FILL IN THE BLANKS BELOW AND SING IT OUT!**

THE TRUE STORY OF THE STAR-SPANGLED BANNER

THE YEAR WAS 1814. The United States was at war with Britain, trying to prove its strength as an independent country. It was called The War of 1812, but it had stretched into years of battles. For the first few years, things were going in America's favor, but in 1814 it looked like the British were winning. They marched into Washington and set fire to the White House and the Capitol building.

Next, the British turned toward Maryland. Their goal was to take **BALTIMORE, AN IMPORTANT SEAPORT**. If the British took control of Baltimore harbor, America would be in big trouble because the British would control many of the goods and supplies going into and out of the country. The people of the United States were nervous and scared.

On September 13, 1814, British warships began bombing Baltimore's **FORT McHENRY**. The fort, which was the only thing stopping the British from entering the city of Baltimore, was under fire for 25 hours straight!

Onboard one of the British ships was an American lawyer named **FRANCIS SCOTT KEY**. He had boarded the ship in order to convince the British to release an American prisoner. He was now stuck on the ship. All he could do was watch the attack on Fort McHenry from the ship's deck.

By the "dawn's early light" of the next morning, Key gazed out across the water and, to his great surprise, he spotted the American flag flying above Fort McHenry.

That meant the fort had not been taken over by the British—**IT HAD NOT SURRENDERED!** America would survive this war!

Key was so inspired by the sight of the flag waving in the distance that he wrote a song on the back of a letter he had in his pocket. Key named the song "The Defence of Fort McHenry." The song was later set to the tune of a popular song of the day and renamed **"THE STAR-SPANGLED BANNER."** It quickly became a hit.

In 1931, well over a hundred years after it was written, the "Star-Spangled Banner" was officially named the national anthem of the United States by President Woodrow Wilson.

SING IT LOUD!

O say can you _____,
by the dawn's early _____
What so proudly we hail'd at the
_____ last gleaming,
Whose broad _____ and bright
_____ through the perilous fight
O'er the ramparts we _____
were so gallantly streaming?
And the _____ red glare,
the bombs _____ in air,
Gave proof through the _____
that our flag was still _____
O _____ does that
star-spangled banner _____

WHAT DOES IT ALL MEAN?

TRY THIS AT HOME! Quick! Take a **POP QUIZ** to see what you really know about the flag of the United States, and **DESIGN YOUR OWN FLAG.**

CHECK OUT THE US FLAG AS IT LOOKS TODAY.
Yes, you've probably seen it a thousand times, but have you ever looked at it really closely?

COLORS OF YOU!
WHAT COLORS WILL YOU USE? COLORS CAN HAVE MEANING, TOO. AT RIGHT ARE SOME MEANINGS CONNECTED TO COLORS.

RED—ENERGY, STRENGTH, POWER, LOVE

ORANGE—ENTHUSIASM, CHEERFULNESS, CREATIVITY

YELLOW—ENERGY, JOY, HAPPINESS, OPTIMISM

PURPLE—ROYALTY, WEALTH, MAGIC, INDEPENDENCE

BLUE—PEACE, TRUST, LOYALTY, WISDOM, CONFIDENCE

GREEN—GROWTH, WELL-BEING, MONEY, NATURE

WHITE—SAFETY, PURITY, INNOCENCE, PEACE

BLACK—POWER, STRENGTH, ELEGANCE, MYSTERY

DESIGN A FLAG TO REPRESENT YOU!

SYMBOLS OF YOU!
WHAT SYMBOLS WILL YOU HAVE ON YOUR FLAG? SYMBOLS CAN SHOW A LOT OF THINGS, ABOUT YOU.

SYMBOLS CAN SHOW:

- how many people are in your family
- what you believe or support
- where you live
- what you like
- your age
- or anything else that is important to you

POP QUIZ

1. How many stars are on the flag?..........

2. How many white stripes are on the flag?..........

3. How many red stripes are on the flag?..........

Answers: 1. There are 50 stars on the American flag today, and each represents a state. The last star was added in 1959 when Hawaii became a state. 2. There are 6 white stripes. 3. There are 7 red stripes. The 13 stripes together symbolize the 13 original colonies.

STAR-SPANGLED

A close-up look at The Star-Spangled Banner

Can you believe that each cotton star on the Star-Spangled Banner is two feet across?

The blue part of the flag is called the canton. It is made of wool dyed blue with indigo.

Count the number of stripes on the original Star-Spangled Banner. The stripes were for each original colony plus Kentucky and Vermont, the next states to join the union. Do you know how many stripes are on the flag today?

This photograph of the Star-Spangled Banner is actually a total of 73 photos carefully pieced together like a puzzle on a computer.

CHECK IT OUT!
FIND MORE FUN FACTS LIKE THESE ON THE INTERACTIVE TOUCH-TABLE IN *THE STAR-SPANGLED BANNER* EXHIBIT AND ONLINE.

FINDS

FLAG FACTS!
- MADE BY MARY PICKERSGILL IN BALTIMORE, MARYLAND, IN JULY-AUGUST 1813
- COMMISSIONED BY MAJOR GEORGE ARMISTEAD, COMMANDER OF FORT MCHENRY
- FIRST LOANED TO THE SMITHSONIAN INSTITUTION IN 1907; CONVERTED TO PERMANENT GIFT IN 1912

The Star-Spangled Banner has been through a lot. Before it was given to the Smithsonian, dozens of patches were sewn on. How many can you find?

Where is the 15th star? Nobody knows. It was cut out of the flag and given away long ago. It may be hidden in someone's attic waiting to be discovered.

Does this flag look short to you? It should. It used to be eight feet longer. Bits and pieces of the Star-Spangled Banner were snipped off and given away as souvenirs!

JOURNAL

What surprised you about the Star-Spangled Banner?

SO, YO TO BE PR

So, you want to be president. **IT'S A BIG JOB**, so first you need to know what will be required of you.

The job of the president of the United States is actually seven jobs rolled into one! Every day the president does most or all of the following jobs:

1. **CHIEF EXECUTIVE**—makes sure the Federal Government runs according to the laws of the United States.

2. **PARTY LEADER**—boosts your political party's ideas, whichever political party you are a member of (Democrat, Republican, or something else).

3. **MANAGER OF THE ECONOMY**—makes sure people have jobs and the United States stays prosperous.

SEE WHAT IT WOULD BE LIKE TO BE PRESIDENT FOR A DAY!

JOURNAL

Which part of the j

Which part of the

I could do that!

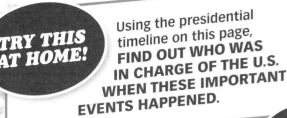

TRY THIS AT HOME!

Using the presidential timeline on this page, FIND OUT WHO WAS IN CHARGE OF THE U.S. WHEN THESE IMPORTANT EVENTS HAPPENED.

POP QUIZ

WHO WAS PRESIDENT WHEN?

1 1803—The Louisiana Purchase doubled the size of the United Sates.

2 1814—The Star-Spangled Banner flew at Fort McHenry in Baltimore, Maryland.

3 1846—The Smithsonian Institution was founded.

4 1865—The slaves were freed by the Thirteenth Amendment to the Constitution.

5 1872—The United States' first National Park, Yellowstone, was established.

6 1903—The Wright Brothers had their first successful flight.

7 1912—The Titanic sank.

8 1932—Amelia Earhart flew across the Atlantic.

9 1959—Alaska and Hawaii become the 49th and 50th states, respectively.

10 1969—The first humans walked on the moon.
(Hint: The man who was president during this event had been sworn in as president in late-January of 1969.)

Answers: 1. Thomas Jefferson 2. James Madison 3. James K. Polk 4. Abraham Lincoln 5. Ulysses S. Grant 6. Theodore Roosevelt 7. William H. Taft 8. Herbert Hoover 9. Dwight D. Eisenhower 10. Richard M. Nixon

PRESIDENT TIMELINE

George Washington (1789-1797)

John Adams (1797-1801)

Thomas Jefferson (1801-1809)

James Madison (1809-1817)

James Monroe (1817-1825)

John Quincy Adams (1825-1829)

Andrew Jackson (1829-1837)

Martin Van Buren (1837-1841)

William H. Harrison (1841)

John Tyler (1841-1845)

James K. Polk (1845-1849)

Zachary Taylor (1849-1850)

Millard Fillmore (1850-1853)

Franklin Pierce (1853-1857)

James Buchanan (1857-1861)

Abraham Lincoln (1861-1865)

Andrew Johnson (1865-1869)

Ulysses S. Grant (1869-1877)

Rutherford B. Hayes (1877-1881)

James A. Garfield (1881)

Chester A. Arthur (1881-1885)

Grover Cleveland (1885-1889)

Benjamin Harrison (1889-1893)

Grover Cleveland (1893-1897)

William McKinley (1897-1901)

Theodore Roosevelt (1901-1909)

William H. Taft (1909-1913)

Woodrow Wilson (1913-1921)

Warren G. Harding (1921-1923)

Calvin Coolidge (1923-1929)

Herbert Hoover (1929-1933)

Franklin D. Roosevelt (1933-1945)

Harry S Truman (1945-1953)

Dwight D. Eisenhower (1953-1961)

John F. Kennedy (1961-1963)

Lyndon B. Johnson (1963-1969)

Richard M. Nixon (1969-1974)

Gerald R. Ford (1974-1977)

Jimmy Carter (1977-1981)

Ronald Reagan (1981-1989)

George H. W. Bush (1989-1993)

Bill Clinton (1993-2001)

George W. Bush (2001-2009)

Barack H. Obama (2009-)

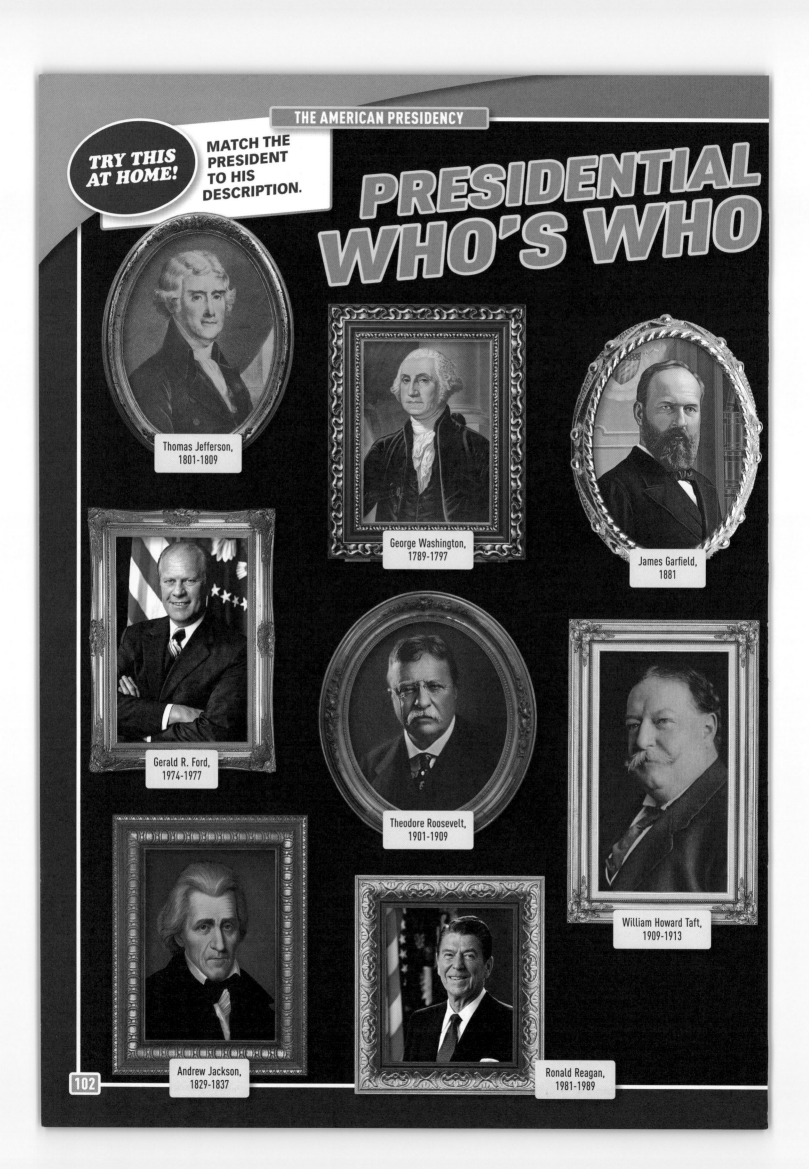

TRY THIS AT HOME!

MATCH THE PRESIDENT TO HIS DESCRIPTION.

PRESIDENTIAL WHO'S WHO

Thomas Jefferson, 1801-1809

George Washington, 1789-1797

James Garfield, 1881

Gerald R. Ford, 1974-1977

Theodore Roosevelt, 1901-1909

William Howard Taft, 1909-1913

Andrew Jackson, 1829-1837

Ronald Reagan, 1981-1989

1 I HAD A PRETTY HOT TEMPER and was famous for dueling (which is just an old-fashioned word for picking fights). I was in over 100 duels in my time and even had a few bullets lodged in my body as a result. Even still, I was pretty popular when I was elected president. Over 20,000 people showed up at my inauguration party at the White House. It was so crowded, I HAD TO SNEAK OUT OF A WINDOW and high-tail it to a hotel for the night!

2 I was a very smart guy. I learned to read when I was three years old. Before becoming president, I was a teacher. At parties, I LIKED TO IMPRESS MY GUESTS by writing with both hands, at the same time, and in two different languages! Unfortunately, I was shot four months after I became president and died from my wounds eleven weeks later.

3 I WAS ONE OF THE MOST ADVENTUROUS AND ATHLETIC presidents. I jogged, played tennis, mountain climbed, boxed, hiked, swam, and more. I was the first president to ride in a car, fly in an airplane, and go underwater in a submarine. After my time in office ended, I went on a year-long collecting expedition in East Africa for the Smithsonian Institution. You can see a white rhino I brought back in the *Hall of Mammals* at the National Museum of Natural History.

4 Yes, I had rotten teeth. But you wouldn't know it because I had many sets of false teeth. They were made out of all sorts of things, including lead, gold, ivory, walrus and elephant tusks, and teeth from a cow, hippopotamus, and even people! Did you know I WAS THE ONLY PRESIDENT WHO DID NOT LIVE IN THE WHITE HOUSE? That's because it wasn't built yet! I picked out the site for the capital of the United States, though—right near my home, Mount Vernon.

5 Like most other presidents, I had many other jobs before I became president. When I was a teenager, I WAS A LIFEGUARD and saved over 70 people from drowning. Another memorable job was that of HOLLYWOOD MOVIE STAR. I starred in more than 50 movies in my younger years. By the time I took the job of president of the United States, I was a few weeks away from my 70th birthday, making me the oldest president in history!

6 I never wanted to be president. I wanted to be a Supreme Court justice. But my wife, Nellie, really wanted to be First Lady, so I ran for her. Being president was a difficult and lonely job, and I ate a lot of food to feel better. I gained 100 pounds when I was president, making me America's heaviest president. I EVEN GOT STUCK IN THE BATHTUB in the White House once! I did eventually make it to the Supreme Court after my term in the White House was finished.

7 I started life as Leslie Lynch King Jr., but when I was two years old my mom remarried and MY NAME WAS OFFICIALLY CHANGED. At the University of Michigan, I WAS MY FOOTBALL TEAM'S MOST VALUABLE PLAYER. I even got offers to play professional football with the Green Bay Packers and the Detroit Lions. I went to law school instead, because I knew I wanted a career in politics.

8 I WAS A MAN OF MANY TALENTS. I am remembered as an inventor, farmer, writer, historian, scientist, musician, linguist, architect, and founder of the University of Virginia. As president, I PURCHASED THE LOUISIANA TERRITORY from France and sent the explorers Lewis and Clark to check out the country's new land out West. They brought back a lot of souvenirs for me, including a few grizzly bears that lived in cages on the White House grounds.

Answers: 1. Andrew Jackson 2. James Garfield 3. Theodore Roosevelt 4. George Washington 5. Ronald Reagan 6. William Howard Taft 7. Gerald R. Ford 8. Thomas Jefferson

WANTED:
FIRST LADY OF THE UNITED STATES

White House seeking First Lady for a four- to eight-year term. First Lady must be wife, daughter, daughter-in-law, niece, or other female relative or friend of the president.

ENDLESS DUTIES INCLUDE:

- **HELPING THE PRESIDENT** win the election by campaigning tirelessly;

- being the White House hostess—**WELCOMING GUESTS** into your home many times a week, throwing fancy parties, and being friendly to all visitors;

- **SUPPORTING CAUSES** and charities of your choosing, setting a good example with your concern for important issues;

- supporting the president's plans and ideas as the chief executive of the United States; staying informed on current issues so you can **OFFER ADVICE** as well;

- being **WILLING TO BE AN EXTREMELY FAMOUS PERSON** in the United States and around the world;

- **CONNECTING WITH PEOPLE** by maintaining a sense of humor, an open and honest attitude, and a true interest in all Americans.

You will not receive payment for the work you do, but you will be provided with a home (the White House), a staff to help you, and other benefits, such as exciting **OPPORTUNITIES TO TRAVEL THE WORLD** and meet all kinds of people.

JOURNAL

Girls, would you want the job of First Lady? Boys, would you take on the responsibilities of a job like this?

What do you think would be some of the fun things about being First Lady?

What do you think would be the worst part about being First Lady?

MEET THE FIRST LADIES

The people who become First Ladies are really not very different from other people, even you!

They have favorite books, favorite TV shows, and favorite colors. They have hobbies and other interests. They come from a variety of backgrounds and went to different kinds of schools. **EACH ONE IS TALENTED IN HER OWN WAY.** Many had careers before they became First Ladies. Meet some First Ladies here, and learn an interesting fact or two about each one.

LOUISA ADAMS: MY HOBBIES INCLUDED PLAYING THE HARP AND RAISING SILKWORMS.

ELIZA JOHNSON: I TAUGHT MY HUSBAND HOW TO READ AND WRITE!

PEGGY TAYLOR: MY HUSBAND AND I LIVED ON THE WESTERN FRONTIER BEFORE COMING TO WASHINGTON. THAT'S WHERE I LEARNED TO SHOOT A GUN.

LOU HOOVER: I GRADUATED FROM STANFORD UNIVERSITY WITH A DEGREE IN GEOLOGY. I ALSO SERVED AS THE PRESIDENT OF THE GIRL SCOUTS. AND ONE MORE THING, I SPOKE CHINESE FLUENTLY.

ELEANOR ROOSEVELT: AS FIRST LADY, I WROTE A DAILY NEWSPAPER COLUMN AND HOSTED A WEEKLY RADIO SHOW.

GRACE COOLIDGE: I WAS A TEACHER AT THE CLARKE SCHOOL FOR THE DEAF.

NANCY REAGAN: BEFORE BECOMING FIRST LADY, I WAS A MOVIE STAR, JUST LIKE MY HUSBAND.

BETTY FORD: I WAS A PROFESSIONAL DANCER WITH THE FAMOUS MARTHA GRAHAM DANCE COMPANY IN NEW YORK CITY.

HILLARY CLINTON: I AM THE ONLY FIRST LADY TO BE ELECTED TO PUBLIC OFFICE—THE UNITED STATES SENATE—AND TO SERVE AS A MEMBER OF THE PRESIDENT'S CABINET—SECRETARY OF STATE.

MICHELLE OBAMA: I GRADUATED FROM PRINCETON UNIVERSITY AND WENT ON TO HARVARD LAW SCHOOL. I BECAME A LAWYER IN CHICAGO.

THAT'S QUITE A DRESS!

TRY THIS IN THE MUSEUM!

Visit the *First Ladies* exhibit. If you were awarding the **PRIZES BELOW**, which dresses and accessories would you give them to? **DRAW THE AWARD WINNERS, OR MAKE NOTES ABOUT WHAT YOU OBSERVE**, in the spaces below.

FANCIEST:

MOST BEAUTIFUL:

MOST COLORFUL:

Frances Cleveland's evening gown from the 1890s

Mamie Eisenhower's evening gown worn in 1957

Jackie Kennedy's silk evening gown worn in 1961

CHECK IT OUT!
FOR MORE PICTURES OF FIRST LADIES' GOWNS TAKE A LOOK ONLINE.

Florence Harding's dress from the 1920s

Nancy Reagan's 1981 inaugural gown

Laura Bush's 2001 inaugural gown

Hillary Clinton's 1993 inaugural gown

Pat Nixon's 1969 inaugural gown

Grace Coolidge's flapper-style dress from the 1920s

DIFFERENT:

WEIRDEST:

BEST OVERALL GOWN:

BEST ACCESSORY:

Ida McKinley's boots

I wonder if they have one in my size?

107

TRY THIS AT HOME!

your mom or dad was the president of the United States. What would that be like? **FILL IN THE BLANKS TO MAKE UP A FUN FIRST KID STORY!**

FIRST KIDS
WHITE H

THE
SIX K
KNEW
HOUS
MA
MATC
HO

TH

Dear .... ,
(name of best friend)

I still can't believe .... is the new
(mom or dad)

president of the United States! Can you? This is going

to be very ....
(adjective)

Yesterday we moved into the White House. Boy, it sure is

different from my home back in ....
(name of your town)

First of all, I think I've counted .... rooms and ....
(number)   (number)

bathrooms! There's also a .... room
(a favorite activity)

and a .... room.
(another favorite activity)

It looks like we're going to be having a lot of parties around

here. I think we should have a sleepover in the ....
(color)

room. We can eat all the .... we want
(food)

and then watch .... in the private
(movie)

White House movie theater.

Write back soon, and tell me what's happening back in

....
(name of your town)

                              Your friend,

                    ....
                              (your name)

FIRST PETS OF THE WHITE HOUSE

Since the very beginning, there have been pets living at the White House—all kinds of pets!

The Obama family dog, Bo, is a fluffy Portuguese water dog.

Theodore Roosevelt's son, Quentin, had a pet macaw named Eli Yale. The Roosevelts also had cats, dogs, snakes, raccoons, and a pony. They practically had a zoo living on the grounds of the White House!

Jimmy Carter's daughter, Amy, had a Siamese cat that she called Misty Malarky Ying Yang. She also was given an elephant that now lives at the National Zoo in Washington, DC.

Calvin Coolidge's wife, Grace, regularly walked her pet raccoon on a leash!

CHECK ALL OF THE ANIMALS BELOW THAT YOU THINK HAVE LIVED AT THE WHITE HOUSE OVER THE YEARS:

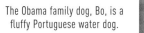

- ☐ cat
- ☐ dog
- ☐ bird
- ☐ hamster
- ☐ rat
- ☐ snake
- ☐ cow
- ☐ horse
- ☐ pony
- ☐ donkey
- ☐ bobcat
- ☐ lion cub
- ☐ antelope

- ☐ wallaby
- ☐ pygmy hippo
- ☐ bear
- ☐ ram
- ☐ goose
- ☐ macaw
- ☐ badger
- ☐ guinea pig
- ☐ elephant
- ☐ hyena

- ☐ bald eagle
- ☐ coyote
- ☐ parrot
- ☐ zebra
- ☐ barn owl
- ☐ lizard
- ☐ rooster
- ☐ raccoon
- ☐ billy goat
- ☐ pig
- ☐ turkey

Did you check them all? You should have, because they all were pets in the White House.

CHECK IT OUT! FIND OUT WHICH PRESIDENTIAL FAMILIES HAD WHICH PETS AT THE PRESIDENTIAL PET MUSEUM!

Korean refugees leave as American soldiers head toward the front lines during the Korean War.

THE PRICE O
AMERI
AT V

Americans have gon
time again.

HERE ARE SOME

- to fight for indep
- to claim more la
- to defend friend the globe
- to protect thems interests around

Each time America history of the Unite the lives of its peop at war by visiting *T* located on 3, East,

KNOW THE LINGO!

the front—the area where opposing armies are located and operating during wartime

home front—this refers to the people at home when a nation is at war

ally—another nation that is on the same side in a war

military—any branch of the armed forces, such as the army, navy, air force, marines, or coast guard

civilian—a person who is not in the military

CHECK IT OUT!
VISIT *THE PRICE OF FREEDOM* GALLERY ONLINE.

US soldiers land on the beach in Normandy, France, on June 6, 1944, during World War II. This invasion to free Europe from Nazi control is known as D-Day.

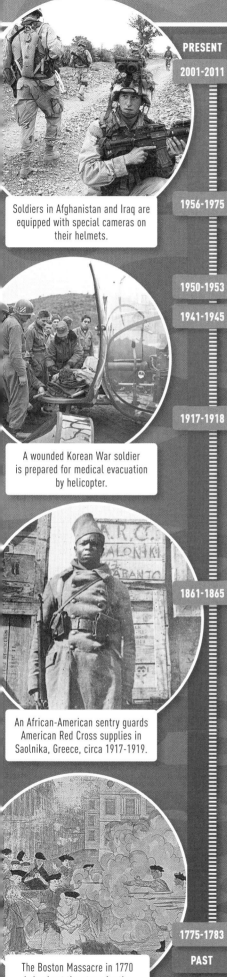

PRESENT

2001-2011

Soldiers in Afghanistan and Iraq are equipped with special cameras on their helmets.

1956-1975

1950-1953

1941-1945

1917-1918

A wounded Korean War soldier is prepared for medical evacuation by helicopter.

1861-1865

An African-American sentry guards American Red Cross supplies in Saolnika, Greece, circa 1917-1919.

1775-1783

PAST

The Boston Massacre in 1770 helped set the stage for the Revolutionary War.

2001-2011 Wars in Afghanistan and Iraq
Americans fought to defend themselves against threats at home as well as in other countries.
American troops involved: over 2 million
Deaths: 6,488

1956-1975 Vietnam War
Americans fought a long, unpopular war against communism and its expansion in Vietnam, a country located in Southeast Asia.
American troops involved: 9,200,000
Deaths: 58,200

1950-1953 Korean War
Americans led efforts to keep communism, a form of government, from spreading in Korea.
American troops involved: 5,720,000
Deaths: 36,576

1941-1945 World War II
Americans joined their allies to defeat powerful countries, known as the Axis powers, that were trying to control as much of the world as they could.
American troops involved: 16,112,566
Deaths: 405,399

1917-1918 World War I
American reluctantly entered Europe's "Great War" and helped its allies claim victory.
American troops involved: 4,734,991
Deaths: 116,516

1861-1865 Civil War
Americans fought each other over preserving their Union and ending slavery.
Troops involved: 3,263,363
Deaths: 529,332

1775-1783 American Revolutionary War
Americans went to war to win their independence from Great Britain.
Troops involved: 217,000
Deaths: 4,435

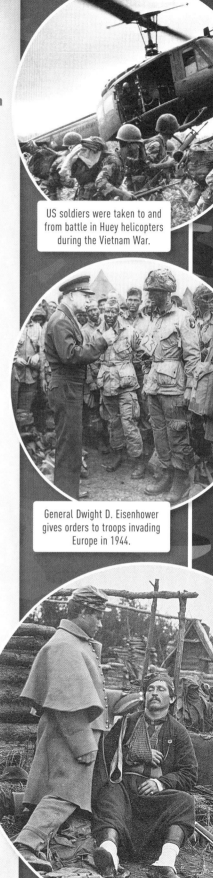

US soldiers were taken to and from battle in Huey helicopters during the Vietnam War.

General Dwight D. Eisenhower gives orders to troops invading Europe in 1944.

The Civil War was the United States' deadliest conflict.

Anthony Sailer wrote many letters home to his wife and son while he was at war in Europe. How do soldiers stay in touch with loved ones today?

Ya Darling:

...ee, is time going slow for us. All tha
...tting down trees for fire wood, and
...re to keep warm, and oh, yes, occa
...omething to eat, but not much. ...
Darling, how is the war progressing?
...news at all. For all we know, the war

It rained all night, but it is bea
I cold. We just took our first sh
England and I miss that dirt; it
warm. Boy, I certainly hope tha
keeps up. A few more weeks of
and I'm sure the Allies will knoc
for good.

April 14,
Ger

Gee Darling, a funny thing happenec
to me the other day. I was walking
through a small village when three
planes came and started to bomb a
strafe this village. I ran into the nea
house for protection, and there I fo
an old German lady and her daught
on their knees praying, crying with
fear, and shaking like leaves. I tried
comfort them, telling them not to k
scared. They felt so much better th
I was there with them, and after th
airplanes left, they tried to give me
and other things to eat to show me
their appreciation, but I refused the
because I'm getting plenty to eat.

INTERVIEW a grandparent, parent, or someone else who is **INTERESTED IN TALKING WITH YOU** about life during wartime, either serving in the **MILITARY** or as a **CIVILIAN**.

WARTIME INTERVIEW

One great way to learn about history is by interviewing people about their life experiences.

Now it's your turn to capture a piece of history! Be sure to **WRITE DOWN** the person's **FULL NAME** and **BIRTH DATE** as well as the date and place of the interview.

Here's what you need →

- In what war and branch of service did you serve?
- What was your rank?
- Where did you serve?
- What was your job?
- Can you tell me about a couple of your most memorable experiences?
- How did you stay in touch with your family?
- Can you describe your living conditions?
- What was it like to come home after the war?
- How did your military experience affect your life?

A LIST OF QUESTIONS TO ASK

Here are some questions you can ask someone who served in the military:

- In what war and branch of service did you serve?
- What was your rank?
- Where did you serve?
- What was your job?
- Can you tell me about a couple of your most memorable experiences?
- How did you stay in touch with your family?
- Can you describe your living conditions?
- What was it like to come home after the war?
- How did your military experience affect your life?

TIP!
ASK THE INTERVIEWEE TO SHARE PHOTOGRAPHS, LETTERS, AND OTHER MEMORABILIA WITH YOU.

A VIDEO OR AUDIO RECORDER (OPTIONAL)

TIP!
BE SURE TO ASK PERMISSION BEFORE RECORDING SOMEONE YOU'RE INTERVIEWING.

A NOTEBOOK FOR JOTTING DOWN NOTES

Here are some questions you can ask a civilian:

- What war did you live through, and where were you living at the time?
- Did you have a job outside of the home during the war? If so, can you tell me about it?
- How did you feel about the war?
- In what ways did the war change your daily life?
- Did you know anyone who served in the war or who was killed or wounded during the war?
- How did you get news about what was happening in the war?

CHECK IT OUT!
FOR MORE INFORMATION ABOUT INTERVIEWING VETERANS, CHECK OUT THE LIBRARY OF CONGRESS' VETERANS HISTORY PROJECT.

TIP!
FOR MORE INDEPTH ANSWERS, TRY ASKING QUESTIONS THAT START WITH "HOW," "WHEN," AND "WHY."

TRY THIS AT HOME!

DO YOU HAVE THE TRAVEL BUG? Where in the United States have you traveled? Where would you like to go? If you live in the United States, **DRAW A STAR** where you live on the map below. **CIRCLE** all the places where you've been in the US. Mark places you'd like to visit with an **ARROW**.

WHERE HAVE YOU BEEN?

Ever since the earliest humans walked the earth, people have been on the move.

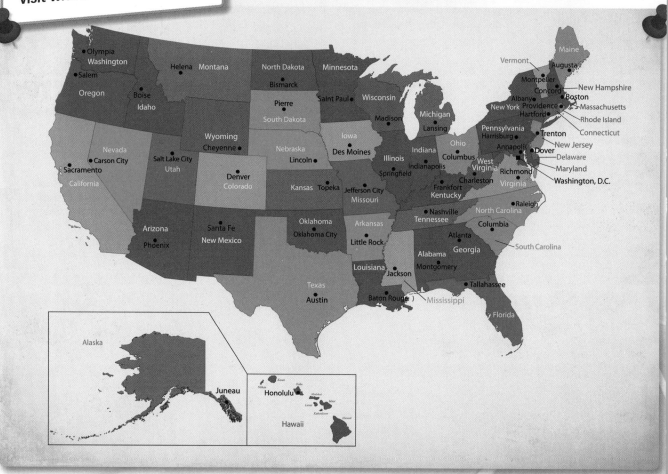

WHY DO PEOPLE MOVE?

People move for a **VARIETY OF REASONS**. Long ago, many people moved to find things they needed to survive—like food, water, and shelter. Today many people move to find better jobs or a better quality of life.

People have always searched for faster and **EASIER WAYS** to get from one place to another. Long ago, they followed paths created by other people or animals. Some paths widened into dirt roads as more people used them. Some were eventually paved over to become the roads we use today.

HOW HAS TRAVEL CHANGED OVER TIME?

Traveling is **NOT SO DIFFICULT FOR US TODAY**, is it? With modern transportation systems, we can travel hundreds, and even thousands, of miles in just a few hours. It would have taken our ancestors weeks or months—sometimes years—to travel the same distances! Back then, few people traveled more than a few dozen miles from where they were born. Better transportation means we can live farther away from stores and other resources. We can stay connected with people near and far.

WHERE ARE YOU GOING?

CHECK ALL OF THE TYPES OF TRANSPORTATION YOU HAVE USED IN YOUR LIFE:

- [ ] car
- [ ] truck
- [ ] van
- [ ] train
- [ ] airplane
- [ ] bus
- [ ] subway
- [ ] bicycle
- [ ] motorcycle
- [ ] tricycle
- [ ] scooter
- [ ] skateboard
- [ ] in-line skates
- [ ] pogo stick
- [ ] skis
- [ ] snowboard
- [ ] sleigh
- [ ] hot-air balloon
- [ ] motor home
- [ ] trailer
- [ ] surfboard
- [ ] sailboat
- [ ] canoe
- [ ] kayak
- [ ] horse
- [ ] wagon
- [ ] tractor
- [ ] streetcar
- [ ] helicopter
- [ ] blimp
- [ ] taxicab
- [ ] wheelchair
- [ ] parachute
- [ ] Segway
- [ ] my own two feet
- [ ] other: ....

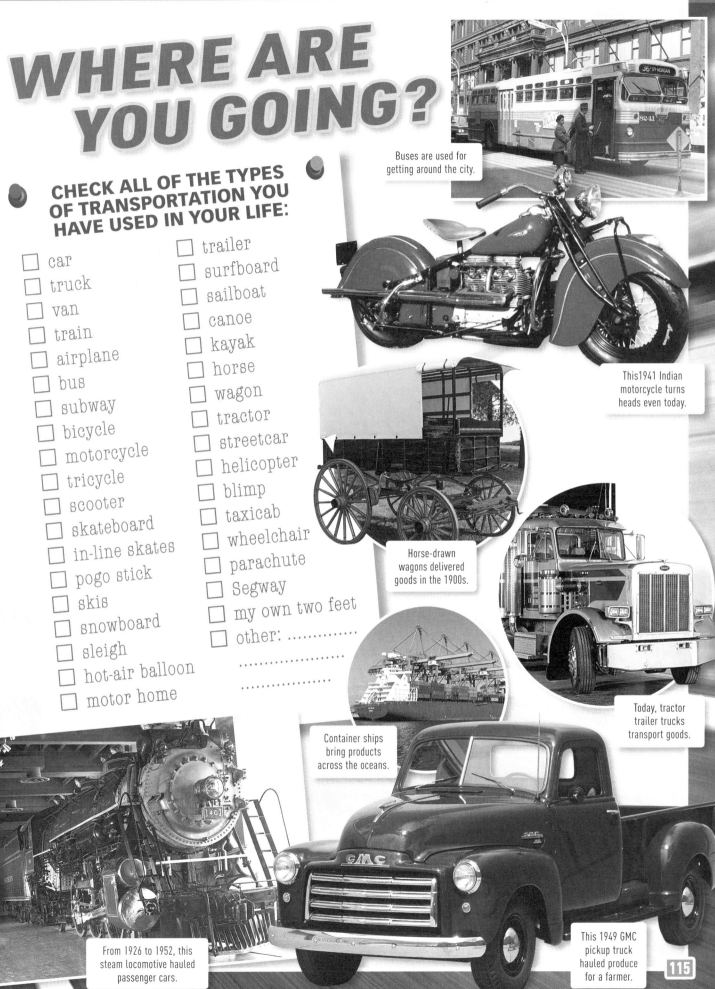

Buses are used for getting around the city.

This 1941 Indian motorcycle turns heads even today.

Horse-drawn wagons delivered goods in the 1900s.

Today, tractor trailer trucks transport goods.

Container ships bring products across the oceans.

From 1926 to 1952, this steam locomotive hauled passenger cars.

This 1949 GMC pickup truck hauled produce for a farmer.

AMERICA'S DOLLHOUSE

TRY THIS IN THE MUSEUM! Use your **MEGA-POWERS** of observation to find the **MINI-TREASURES** in the **DOLLS' HOUSE**.

FAITH BRADFORD loved all things miniature. When she was a kid in the 1890's, she **INHERITED** her older sister's four-room dollhouse and the furniture and dolls that went along with it. She **PLAYED** with the dollhouse so much that it fell apart. So, she started using the shelves in her **BEDROOM CLOSET** as rooms for her miniature dolls and furniture collection. In her imagination, the dollhouse was the home of the **DOLL FAMILY**—Mr. and Mrs. Peter Doll and their ten children. She called it the **DOLLS' HOUSE**.

Faith Bradford shares her prized possession with a young Smithsonian visitor in 1967. For years, the Dolls' House was inspected and cleaned by Ms. Bradford, and each December she decorated it for the holidays.

CHECK THESE OFF WHEN YOU FIND THEM:

- [ ] Grandmother Doll is snoozing in the guest room.
- [ ] Is that a sculpture of George Washington up in the attic?
- [ ] Alice Doll has her own doll, of course!
- [ ] Shh! The baby twins, Jimmy and Timmy, are asleep in their bassinet.
- [ ] What's for dinner?
- [ ] Gadsby, the butler, is preparing for dinner in the pantry.
- [ ] Is that a bear-skin rug in the drawing room?
- [ ] A dollhouse in the Dolls' House!
- [ ] A "new" Hoover vacuum cleaner stands upright in a corner.

The drawing room

Guest bathroom

THE MINIATURE WORLD OF FAITH BRADFORD

As she grew older, Faith did not **GROW OUT** of her hobby of collecting tiny household items. She continued to find pieces for her collection in toy and specialty stores. She also **RECEIVED** pieces as **GIFTS** and made pieces herself with everyday items like buttons.

In 1951, when Faith Bradford was in her seventies, she **DONATED** the Dolls' House and her entire collection of miniature dolls, furniture, and accessories to the Smithsonian Institution. Today it continues to **ATTRACT KIDS** of all ages.

Welcome to the **MINIATURE WORLD** of Faith Bradford!

Peter Jr.'s room

Fish tank

DOLLHOUSE FACTS:

- 23 rooms
- 2 parents (Peter and Rose Doll)
- 10 children (twins Jimmy & Timmy, twins Carol & Lucy, Christopher, Ann, David, Alice, Robin, Peter Jr.)
- 2 grandparents
- 5 servants
- 20 pets

The sewing room

Mr. Doll's typewriter

Whose bicycle is this?

HOW MANY PETS CAN YOU SPOT?

An entire house in a museum?
Only at the Smithsonian!

Meet five
during

❶ The Choate Far
Colonists 1757-
This was the first fa
house. Abraham Ch
house built for his v

❷ The Dodges an
Revolutionaries

Bethiah a
lived in t
Revolutio
an office
militia, fe
Bunker H
an enslav
named C
lived in t
Chance v
in Massa
to compl
that his
with the

Bethiah Dodge used
tools like these to make
lace in her home.

❸ The Caldwells–
1836-1865
Josiah and Lucy Ca
in the house with t
Margaret. They we
reformers—people
to change things. T
wanted to end slav
the president of th
Anti-Slavery Societ
meetings in the pa
sitting room, of the

THE STORY OF MY HOME

TRY THIS AT HOME! What is the story of **YOUR HOME**? Ask your parents or another adult you live with to help you **LEARN MORE ABOUT YOUR HOME**.

Like **DETECTIVES**, historians gather information from all kinds of sources. **DOCUMENTS** on file in **TOWN HALLS** or libraries can offer clues. These can be anything from **PHOTOGRAPHS**, newspaper articles, and diaries to city directories, **MAPS**, wills, and **DEEDS** (which show who owns a house or other kind of property). What can you find out about **YOUR HOME?**

DRAW A BIRD'S-EYE VIEW OR FLOOR PLAN THAT SHOWS THE ROOMS ON EACH FLOOR OF YOUR HOME.

LIST THE DIFFERENT ROOMS IN YOUR HOME.

DRAW A PICTURE OF YOUR HOME, ADDING DETAILS THAT WILL HELP TELL THE STORY OF WHO LIVES IN YOUR HOME.

My address: ....

I have lived in this home for .... years.

I think my house was built in the year ....

I live in (circle one): an apartment / a single-family home / a multi-family home

I live in (circle one or more): the city / the country / the suburbs / a neighborhood

CHECK IT OUT!
EXPLORE THE
ONLINE EXHIBIT.

Ar
unde
In t
lea
Unite
you
st

© The Mup

Alexander Graham

Can you imagine what life
telephones? How would yo
How would you talk to rela
telephone in the 1870s cha
Inventor Alexander Graham
how to send sounds, like t
he succeeded in sending h
laboratory. The first teleph
Thomas Watson, was short
Bell: "Mr. Watson, come he

How would your life be d

STORIES

Teddy Bear, around 1903

Do you have a favorite stuffed animal? How about a teddy bear? For more than a century, the teddy bear has been one of the most popular toys of childhood. It all started with a president of the United States. That's right, in 1902, President Theodore Roosevelt was on a bear hunt. It had gone on for days with no success. Finally, an old, tired bear was captured and offered up to the president to shoot as a hunting trophy. President Roosevelt refused. The story of the spared bear became well-known when Clifford Berryman, a cartoonist for the *Washington Post*, drew a comic of the event. The cartoon gave a Brooklyn candy store owner an idea. He created a stuffed bear and named it Teddy, after the president. The "Teddy Bear" was born and has been a favorite of kids ever since.

Do you have a Teddy Bear?

Dorothy's Ruby Slippers™, 1938

It's hard to imagine a time when all movies were in black-and-white. One of the first movie to be filmed in color was *The Wizard of Oz*, made by MGM in 1939. These shoes were worn by the lead character Dorothy played by the 16-year-old star Judy Garland. In the original book, by L. Frank Baum, Dorothy's magical slippers were silver. They were changed to ruby red in the movie so they could be seen clearly against the yellow-brick road. These were just one of many pairs of ruby slippers Judy Garland wore during the filming of *The Wizard of Oz*. They were most likely the pair she wore when filming the dance numbers.

Have you seen *The Wizard of Oz*?

Crayola Crayons, about 1903

How many crayons do you suppose you've scribbled with in your lifetime? Probably boxes and boxes of them, like most kids. Did you know that the Crayola crayon was invented more than 110 years ago? Talk about staying power! The Crayola crayon was invented by the Binney & Smith Company of Easton, Pennsylvania. But what does "Crayola" mean? The name for the waxy coloring stick comes from the French word *craie* (sounds like *cray*), which means "chalk," and *ola* from "oleaginous," which means oily. Some of the earliest Crayola crayons came in a set of 28 colors, including celestial blue, golden ochre, rose pink, and burnt sienna. Today you can find inventive Crayola colors such as jazzberry jam, mango tango, wild blue yonder, eggplant, cotton candy, magic mint, outer space, manatee, fuzzy wuzzy brown, purple mountain's majesty, and macaroni and cheese.

What color is your favorite? If you were asked to name a new color, what would it be?

The Nintendo Game Boy, a hit in 1989

IT'S POP CULTUR
KID!

What's pop cult
It's short for "po
culture," and it in
all of the things th
popular at a certa
and in a certain p

WORLD'S LARGEST SELLING
COMIC MAGAZINE!

ACTION COMICS JAN.

An Action Comics book form 1940 features the caped superhero, Superman.

Droids C-3PO and R2-D2,
popular since the 1977
release of Star Wars

Pop culture can include:
- popular TV shows;
- the coolest toys and games;
- the most famous movie stars;
- best-selling clothing;
- favorite sayings of the day; and
- common ideas and attitudes of the time.

Pop culture might not be focused on the most earth-shaking, history-making events in a country, but it can give us an idea of what's popular in the day-to-day lives of regular people.

TRY THIS AT HOME!

DESIGN YOUR OWN POP-CULTURE LUNCH BOX. Illustrate the lunch box below with something popular from your life today.

1983 *Sesame Street* lunchbox, based on television show

Fat Albert and the Cosby Kids lunchbox, based on an aminated TV series in the 1970s and 80s

What do you use to carry your lunch to school?

What does your lunch container say about your taste in pop culture? Yes, even lunch boxes can give you an idea of what has been popular with kids over the past half-century.

YOUR OWN LUNCH BOX:

Disney school bus lunchbox, a favorite in 1961

Mulan lunchbox, based on the hit 1998 Disney movie

DID YOU KNOW? YOU CAN SEE DOZENS OF LUNCH BOXES FROM THE SMITHSONIAN'S COLLECTION IN THE STARS AND STRIPES CAFE, ON THE MUSEUM'S LOWER LEVEL.

Lost in Space lunchbox, based on a popular science-fiction program

Ask your parents and grandparents if they remember any of the lunch boxes on this page. They probably will!

POP QUIZ

Woody Woodpecker lunchbox, based on a cartoon popular in the 1960s

TAKE A LOOK AT THE LUNCH BOXES ON THIS PAGE.

Which one do you think was the most popular lunch box of all time?

Answer: The Disney School Bus was the best-selling lunch box ever, with more than 9 million sold!

NATIONAL MUSEUM OF AMERICAN HISTORY. Then write a few lines to **YOURSELF** about your visit. What do you want to **REMEMBER**?

The National Museum of American History

What were some of your favorite stories from the National Museum of American History?

George Washington's portrait, painted by Rembrandt Peale

Dear Me,

_____

_____

_____

_____

_____

_____

Love, Me

Me!
My street!
My town!
My country!

AMERICAN HISTORY?

THINK FAST!

20 QUESTIONS: After your visit to the National Museum of American History, answer these questions as fast as you can!

Baseball, signed by Babe Ruth in 1929

1. Was this your first time visiting the Smithsonian's National Museum of American History?   YES/NO

2. How long were you at the museum?

....

4. Did you see Bud, the bulldog, and the automobile he rode in across the United States in 1903?   YES/NO

5. Have you tried singing the "Star-Spangled Banner" yet?   YES/NO

6. What was your favorite exhibit?

....

7. What is one thing that you will remember from *The Price of Freedom* exhibit?

....

8. Did you go aboard the "L" train in the *America on the Move* exhibit?   YES/NO

3. Did you see Dorothy's ruby slippers?   YES/NO

18. Did you find any new exhibits?   YES/NO

9. Which was your favorite gown in the *First Ladies* exhibit?

....

10. Did you find out who lived in the house from Elm Street?   YES/NO

11. Did you track down the lunch box collection?   YES/NO

12. What do you want to know about your ancestors?

....

13. Did you use the touch board in *The Star-Spangled Banner* exhibit?   YES/NO

14. Did you take a close look at Kermit the Frog?   YES/NO

15. What was one cool thing you saw on the *Artifact Walls*?

....

16. Did you wonder what life would have been like way back then?   YES/NO

17. Did you wonder what it would have been like to be the president of the United States?   YES/NO

20. Did you think about any stories from your past?   YES/NO

19. Did you stare at the details of the Dolls' House?   YES/NO

WHAT'S NEW?
THE NATIONAL MUSEUM OF AMERICAN HISTORY IS ALWAYS MAKING IMPROVEMENTS. THAT MEANS THERE IS ALWAYS SOMETHING NEW TO DISCOVER AT THE MUSEUM. YOU CAN KEEP UP TO-DATE WITH ALL THE LATEST AND GREATEST EXHIBITS BY VISITING US ONLINE.

Prince's Yellow Cloud guitar, designed by the musician

ADDITIONAL RESOURCES

For more activities and information related to the Smithsonian Institution visit the official website for *Awesome Adventures at the Smithsonian*. smithsonianeducation.org/officialkidsguide

Looking for more Smithsonian museums to explore?
There are 16, other than the three covered *in the Official Kids Guide*, located on or near the National Mall and in the Washington, DC, area, and even a couple in New York City! Visit the Smithsonian's website, www.si.edu, for details.

On or near the National Mall, Washington, DC
- Arthur M. Sackler Gallery
- Freer Gallery of Art
- Hirshhorn Museum and Sculpture Garden
- National Museum of African American History and Culture (open 2015)
- National Museum of African Art
- National Museum of the American Indian
- National Portrait Gallery
- National Postal Museum
- Renwick Gallery of the Smithsonian American Art Museum
- Smithsonian American Art Museum
- Smithsonian Institution Building, "The Castle"

In the Washington, DC Metro Area
- Anacostia Community Museum
- National Zoological Park
- Steven F. Udvar-Hazy Center, National Air and Space Museum

In New York City
- Cooper-Hewitt, National Design Museum
- George Gustave Heye Center, National Museum of the American Indian

ACKNOWLEDGMENTS

I would like to thank the many individuals who provided invaluable assistance and guidance in helping to make this book come to fruition.

First, I wish to thank Smithsonian Books staff. Christina Wiginton, my talented editor, who kept me on track and patiently walked me through the process of creating a book—You knew exactly what I needed, whether it was a little encouragement, a deadline, or just an adult conversation during my lunch break. Carolyn Gleason, the director of Smithsonian Books, who made this idea a reality—Thank you for giving me this opportunity. Caroline Newman, former executive editor of Smithsonian Books, whose initial enthusiasm for this book meant the world to me—I wish you could be here to see the finished product. Many thanks also to Matt Litts, marketing manager, who made sure kids, parents, and teachers found out about this book.

I wish to thank Drew McGovern and Liz Wiffen of Punch Bowl Design who made my vision for this book come to life with pages packed with energy and excitement, Jean Crawford, who polished my written work and made it shine, and Amy Pastan, who tracked down the hundreds of fantastic images needed to make this book so fun to explore.

Many thanks to Nina Fasulo and Polly Litts for their careful review of the layouts. Having feedback from kids like you is one of the things that helped make this book so great!

I am also indebted to all of the hardworking Smithsonian staff who supported this project by providing thoughtful feedback on the manuscript and answering my many questions. I would particularly like to thank Julia Garcia, Carrie Kotcho, and Jenny Wei at the National Museum of American History; Bill Watson, Amy Bolton, Gale Robertson, Matt Carrano, Nate Erwin, and Liz Cottrell at the National Museum of Natural History; and Maureen Kerr, Tim Rhue, Michael Huslander, and Beth Wilson at the National Air and Space Museum.

The collective experience and wisdom of friends and colleagues shared with me added another dimension to this book, and I am especially grateful to the following for their contribution: National Air and Space Museum docent, Bobbe Dyke, who has been giving great tours of the museum since it opened in 1976—Thanks for sharing your depth of knowledge with me. National Air and Space Museum Explainers, Jamila Arnolia and Andrew Yu, who helped write the pages explaining how things fly here on Earth and in space. Apollo astronaut Alan Bean, who told me his stories about space travel and walking on the moon—It was a great privilege to speak with you. Lieutenant Commander Kevin Chlan of the United States Navy, an old friend and inspiring person— Thank you for sharing your experiences as a Navy pilot and thank you for your service. Regis Bobonis, Sr., a wealth of information on the history of the Tuskegee Airmen, and Kim Mudd for helping me connect with him.

To my family, friends, and colleagues, I wish to extend a special thank you for your encouragement every step of the way: My husband, Gideon, my coach, encourager, and true partner in this project and in life. Dad and Sharan, whose confidence in me has spurred me on to follow my dreams. Mom and Daddy Ron, always my most vocal cheerleaders. My grandfather, Anthony Sailer, whose letters from WWII appear in this book—You were a true light in my life. My sisters and brothers, Brad & Amy, Rebecca & Richie, Myra & Tim, Gwen & Bobby, Rosemary & Aaron—I love you all so much! Myra Kushon, my talented photographer sister, for a fun photo session and a head shot I really like. My friends and colleagues at Manor School, and the kids and families of Room 5—You inspire me in all I do. Thank you especially to my students who helped me think of interview questions, reviewed page designs, and listened to my many museum stories. My friends and colleagues at the National Museum of Natural History, especially Margery Gordon, Harold Banks, Amy Bolton, Rusty Russell, and Berna Onat—I loved working with you at my favorite museum on the planet.

Dedication: For my dad, Paul Belo, who introduced me to the Smithsonian museums at a young age.

This book may be purchased for educational, business, or sales promotional use. For information, please write:
Special Markets Department
Smithsonian Books
P. O. Box 37012, MRC 513
Washington, DC 20013

Published by Smithsonian Books
Director: Carolyn Gleason
Editor: Christina Wiginton
Editorial Assistants: Jane Gardner, Ashley Montague, and Danielle Villalovos

Edited by Jean Crawford
Designed by Punch Bowl Design
Photo Research by Amy Pastan

Library of Congress Cataloging-in-Publication Data

Smithsonian Institution.
Awesome adventures at the Smithsonian : the official kids guide to the Smithsonian Institution / Emily B. Korrell.
pages cm
Summary: "Kid friendly guidebook to three major Smithsonian museums: The National Air and Space Museum, The National Museum of Natural History, and the National Museum of American History"-- Provided by publisher.

ISBN 978-1-58834-349-9 (pbk.)

1. National Air and Space Museum--Juvenile literature.
2. National Museum of Natural History (U.S.)--Juvenile literature.
3. Science museums--Washington (D.C.)--Guidebooks--Juvenile literature.
4. National Museum of American History (U.S.)--Juvenile literature.
5. Washington (D.C.)--Guidebooks--Juvenile literature. I. Korrell, Emily B. II. Title.

Q105.U52S65 2013
069.09753--dc23

2012029119

Manufactured in China by Oceanic Graphic Printing

17 16 15 14 13   5 4 3 2 1

For permission to reproduce illustrations appearing in this book, please correspond directly with the owners of the works, as seen below. Smithsonian Books does not retain reproduction rights for these images individually, or maintain a file of addresses for sources.

Photo credits